Positive Approaches to Change

Positive Approaches to Change

Applications of Solutions Focus and Appreciative Inquiry at Work

Edited by
Mark McKergow and Jenny Clarke

Solutions Focus at Work Series

solutions
books

First published in Great Britain in 2005 by
SolutionsBooks
26 Christchurch Road
Cheltenham
GL50 2PL
United Kingdom
www.solutionsbooks.com

UK ISBN 0 954 9749 0 5

Cover design by
Cathi Stevenson

Design, typesetting and production by
Action Publishing Technology Ltd

Printed in Great Britain by
Action Publishing Technology Ltd, Gloucester GL1 5SR

Contents

Acknowledgements   ix

The New Wave of Change is in SolutionsBooks!   xi

Editors' Introduction to the SolutionsBooks edition   xiii

Positive Approaches to Organisations and People   1
Mark McKergow
Solutions Focus, Appreciative Inquiry and Positive Psychology
compared in a new introduction to this collection

Dancing the Solution Focused Shuffle!   13
Louis Cauffman
What is a Solutions Focused approach? It's much more
than just acting positively ...

Appreciative Inquiry: Social Construction in Practice   25
Sheila McNamee
Creating new organisational realities together – theory
meets practice

Team Remotivation   39
John Henden
Getting going in the face of mass redundancy and adversity
– a practical case

About Solutions Focused Scaling – 10 minutes for
performance and learning   53
Peter Szabó
Simple ways to make the most of learning opportunities in
the workplace

Solution Focused Reflecting Teams in Action 67
Harry Norman with Tim Pidsley and Michael Hjerth
A flexible format for surfacing the resources and knowledge
present within a team

Solution Focused Rating (SFR): New Ways in Performance
Appraisal 81
Günter Lueger
A novel yet simple approach for building solutions talk within
an appraisal interview

Organisational Constellations meets Appreciative Inquiry 93
Sue Abbotson and Patricia Lustig
A creative experiment in integrating two organisational
transformation (OT) disciplines

Solution Focused Strategic Planning 107
Jim Mortensen
US Government facilitators try it out and give their verdict

Making Competency Management Work: Use What is There! 121
Gwenda Schlundt Bodien and Coert Visser
How to devise a system of management while staying both
solutions focused and client directed

Solution Focused Feedback in Management Development 131
Peter Röhrig
The value of SF conversations using criticism as well as praise for
learning

How to Improve your Tennis, your Management Skills 141
and your Organisation's results
Paul Z Jackson
Case study and research on the impact of Solutions Focused
coaching in Walkers Snackfoods

Dreams do Come True 155
Patricia Lustig
Community building with Appreciative Inquiry in a small
Nepalese village

Reviews

Authentic Happiness: Using the New Positive Psychology   161
to Realise Your Potential for Lasting Fulfilment by Martin
Seligman, review by Coert Visser

The Skaleboard: A tangible tool for coaching and   164
management from SolutionSurfers, Switzerland,
review by Kirsten Dierolf

The Solutions Focus: The SIMPLE Way to Positive   166
Change by Paul Z Jackson and Mark McKergow, review
by Coert Visser

Solution Focused Coaching: Managing people in a   169
complex world by Jane Greene and Antony M Grant,
review by Terry Gibson

About AMED   171
About Organisations & People   173
About SOL   175

Index   177

Acknowledgements

We would like to thank AMED for publishing these pieces originally and for their agreement to publish this collection. Terry Gibson, managing editor of Organisations & People, was instrumental in suggesting the idea of a special issue, which led to much of this work being produced.

Our thanks go to all the authors for agreeing to this new publication. We thank Harry Norman for his help in organising the SOL 2003 conference, the source of much of the material, as well as his continuing role with us in the Bristol Solutions Group. Other BSG colleagues (John Henden, Kate Hart and Alasdair MacDonald) have also been a long way with us on the journey towards skilful SF work. Thanks to our colleagues at The Solutions Focus, Paul Z Jackson and Janine Waldman, for their continuing collaboration and to the organisers of subsequent SOL conferences (Michael Hjerth and the Stockholm 2004 team, and Peter Szabó and colleagues for Interlaken 2005). These forums for sharing and building Solutions Focused practice are a central aspect to the development of our field.

The creation of this book has been eased by the skill and patience of Miles Bailey, Fiona Thornton and the team at Action Publishing Technology.

The New Wave of Change is in SolutionsBooks!

In the 1960s, the legendary record label Impulse! launched itself with the motto 'The new wave of jazz is on Impulse!'. The label became the home of legends like John Coltrane and Charles Mingus, and led the way for a whole movement of new musical forms and talent.

In the same way, we now announce that the new wave of change is in SolutionsBooks! We will be promoting the developing movement around Solutions Focus and other positive, minimal change technologies including narrative and Appreciative Inquiry, which value simplicity and pragmatism over complex models and ill-founded theory.

This new wave is not not simply another model for change – it is a different *kind* of approach. We are not interested in finding grand designs. Instead, we seek ways to find the direct routes to progress, to explore the fine line between what matters and what can be overlooked, to help people and organisations move forwards in a complex and fluid world.

Solutions Focus is built on the successful field of Solution Focused Brief Therapy (SFBT) as developed by Steve de Shazer and Insoo Kim Berg at the Brief Family Therapy Center, Milwaukee. Over the past fifteen years SFBT practitioners have discovered the power of finding what works, staying at the surface, careful listening and building on small successes, and bypassing conventional therapeutic tools such as diagnosis, cause analysis, 'talking through' the problem and searching for repressed feelings and thoughts.

This radically simple, skilful and subtle practice is found in randomised controlled studies to give as good or better results than more conventional methods, but in less time and with greater satisfaction from clients. Practitioners report fewer features of burn-out than with other approaches. We seek to continue this movement into the worlds of organisations, businesses and other settings.

Some people have found the ideas presented here to be simplistic – nice and positive, just like PollyAnna. We think this misses the point: simple is *not* simplistic. To be less simple, to take less direct routes involving a priori problem analysis, weakness diagnosis and any of the other myriad potential excursions and pitfalls, is to risk at best expending more resources and time than necessary, and at worst spreading confusion and making any problems significantly worse.

Ludwig Wittgenstein wrote that the aim of philosophy was 'to show the fly the way out of the fly-bottle'. In promoting the new wave of change, our aim is show how simplicity and clarity can minimise confusion and futile effort. Readers will be better equipped to find their own ways out of bottles.

Mark McKergow and Jenny Clarke
SolutionsBooks
www.solutionsbooks.com

Editors' Introduction to the SolutionsBooks edition

This book is a collection of pieces which originally appeared in Organisations & People, the official journal of the Association for Management Education and Development (AMED). Many first appeared in a special issue, Volume 10 Number 4 (November 2003), guest-edited by us and entitled *Positive Approaches to Change*. To these have been added two extra articles from earlier issues, and a new introduction giving a more detailed comparison between Solutions Focus, Appreciative Inquiry and positive psychology.

This collection represents the first collection of writing on applications of Solutions Focus (SF) in organisational and management work. Louis Cauffman introduces the SF approach with respect to coaching and other interactions. John Henden's work on team remotivation provides a detailed account of an effective half-day's facilitation. Peter Szabó shows how the 'unreasonably effective' scaling method can produce results in the shortest of timescales.

Harry Norman, Michael Hjerth and Tim Pidsley show how the Solution Focused Reflecting Team method is being used internationally for effective wisdom-sharing and team discussions. Günter Lueger's fascinating work on revitalising performance appraisal discussions shows how a small adjustment can open the door to vitally different conversations and results, and Jim Mortensen shares his practical research on using SF as a strategic planning approach within the US Government.

Competency management is the subject of Coert Visser and Gwenda Schlundt Bodien's account of a project where balancing their customer's views with their own proved key to the project's success. Peter Röhrig looks at using SF as a feedback tool in management development, and Paul Z Jackson shares the story and results of a major SF coaching initiative within a large organisation.

Appreciative Inquiry (Ai) is discussed here too. Sheila McNamee clearly describes the way Ai relates to ideas of social construction, and Patricia Lustig's account of her community development work in Nepal sits well alongside her innovative account with Sue Abbotson of combining organisational constellations work with Ai.

This collection is completed with book and resource reviews of some key works in the field – *The Solutions Focus* by Paul Z Jackson and Mark McKergow, *Authentic Happiness* by Martin Seligman, and Anthony Grant and Jane Greene's *Solution Focused Coaching*. *The Skaleboard*, a coaching aid for promoting SF conversations, is also reviewed.

Most of these pieces emerged from presentations and workshops at the SOL 2003 conference (Solutions in Organisations Linkup) in Bristol, UK. For more information on this and future SOL conferences, visit www.solworld.org.

Positive Approaches to Organisations and People:

Solutions Focus, Appreciative Inquiry and Positive Psychology compared

Mark McKergow

You may be thinking that using a positive approach is mind-bogglingly obvious. Who in their right mind would use a 'negative' approach? Under that name, probably no-one. But many of the roots of psychology and psychotherapy take, implicitly, such an approach.

Minus and plus

Conventional psychology has concerned itself with identifying and relieving disorders – stress, depression, disfunction and many more. We have experts on hand who can spot a whole range of defined conditions – for example Attention Deficit Disorder – and are familiar with the range of treatments which can be applied. And we have all heard how 'talking through' a problem and 'working through' the associated negative emotions is, in some eyes, a key step to healing.

Similar analysis is found in organisations. Ed Schein, the father of process consulting, states at the start of his classic book on the subject:

> Managers often do not know what is wrong and need special help in diagnosing what their problems actually are. (*Schein 1988:10*)

The implication is clear – it is important to know what the problem actually is in order to solve it. This route is also implied in the medical model – the doctor has to decide what's wrong with you, and can only then provide an appropriate treatment, defined by and matched to the disease concerned.

This thinking runs very deep in conventional wisdom and folk psychology. It is also found in some more modern ideas in organisational and personal change. For example, one provider of neurolinguistic programming (NLP) coach training states that

> It is very likely that when a client seeks out a Coach for a specific issue, the blocks to them achieving their outcomes may well be rooted in past events. An NLP Coach has access to a vast array of tools to help clear such blocks. Coaches who are not trained in NLP will generally not have these skills. (*ITS, 2004*)

Once again, we see the negative approach in action. There are 'blocks', perhaps rooted in past events, which must be fixed – by the cleverly trained coach. The central aim is to discover the cause of the problem and remove it.

Positive routes

What are the alternatives? In this book you will find reference to three different positive approaches – positive psychology, Appreciative Inquiry and Solutions Focus. These traditions all, in different ways, assert the value of looking not at disorder, problems, causes and weaknesses, but being concerned instead with what is useful, functional and desired. If we can know more about this, then perhaps progress can be made without seeing people and organisations as things that need to be 'fixed'.

All three approaches are rooted in years of application and research. All have been shown to be effective in action, in organisational work and elsewhere. All share an interest in focusing on what already works rather than on what the problems may be.

This is not to say that people don't have problems – clearly they do, and they want to be rid of them. But what all these approaches advise, in their different ways, is that identifying the *problem* is less of a guide to making progress than focusing elsewhere – on strengths, on what people *want*, on what can already be discovered about that.

Some would argue that these are two sides of the same coin. I disagree. If you would like to get a small insight into the differences, try asking someone what they are doing wrong and notice the response. Then some time later ask them what they are doing right, even if they are in a difficult situation. The response is different – often dramatically so.

Getting interested in what's wrong is like trying to travel from London to New York by first listing and examining all the things which make that journey hard or impossible – a depressing, difficult and futile process, compared to phoning the travel agent to find the latest travel possibilities.

So what are the key factors which distinguish these three strands of positive approach?

Positive psychology

Positive psychology is a growing field, applying the methods and tools of conventional psychology to strengths rather than weaknesses. The discipline now centres on the study of positive emotion, positive character traits, and positive institutions. Martin Seligman's books *Learned Optimism* and *Authentic Happiness* are important texts, while one book to focus on organisations is Marcus Buckingham and Donald O Clifton's *Now, Discover Your Strengths*. You will find *Authentic Happiness* reviewed later in this book.

Seligman has recently been president of the American Psychological Society. He was struck by the focus of his discipline on disease, stress, mental illness and disorder. In contrast, little research had been done into living a healthy life, happiness, resilience and other positive aspects of the mind. Seligman, Mihalyi

Czikszentmihalyi (known for his work on flow states) and others are now applying the armoury of psychology to strengths, positive emotions and useful character traits.

In moving the psychological profession's paradigm away from pathology and mental illness towards positive emotion, strengths and virtues, the focus of positive psychologists is on finding ways to reveal these aspects by conventional means – questionnaires, instruments and statistical research. Signature strengths can be scientifically identified and positive emotions measured, it is said, to improve the world around us and reach new levels of performance. A glance at Seligman's website www.authentichappiness.org reveals over twenty psychological instruments now waiting to measure diverse positive aspects of life – from Strengths to Satisfaction, Gratitude to Grit.

From an organisational perspective, Buckingham and Clifton take an interesting and provocative view of people development:

> Most organisations take their employees' strengths for granted and focus on minimising their weaknesses. They become expert in those areas where their employees struggle, delicately rename these 'skill gaps' or 'areas of opportunity', and then pack them off to training classes so the weakness can be fixed. This approach is occasionally necessary: If an employee always alienates those around him, some sensitivity training can help; likewise, a remedial communication class can benefit an employee who happens to be smart but inarticulate. But this isn't development, it's damage control. And by itself damage control is a poor strategy for elevating either the employee or the organisation to world-class performance. (*Buckingham and Clifton 2002*)

The power of personal strengths in organisational life has also been noticed by Dr John Hunt of London Business School. He writes (in Buckingham and Clifton):

> Concentrating on people's strengths . . . This, and only this, will be the major differentiator for organisations in the future.

Veteran business guru Peter Drucker adds that:

> Most people do not know what their strengths are. When you ask them, they look at you with a blank stare, or they respond in terms of subject knowledge, which is the wrong answer.

Focusing on personal strengths may well be key in forming a new view towards organisational life, change and development. But is this classical psychology methodology – using 'instruments' (a term borrowed from the vocabulary of 'hard' science like physics and chemistry) to 'scientifically' measure an individual's positive qualities – the only way to proceed? There are at least two alternative approaches, based on a more systemic and dynamic view of people, language and behaviour.

Social construction and the interactional view

Appreciative Inquiry and Solutions Focus take a less certain, more exploratory view of people and organisations. Though these traditions seem to have developed independently, they are both interested in how behaviour and language emerge from context (the specific circumstances in which they happen), and how meaning is constructed socially in interactions between people

This moves the centre of attention away from instruments and expert-defined strengths, towards the way in which conversations themselves lead to change. Rather than seek an 'official definition' of happiness, for example, it may be more interesting to see how the word is used in context, and therefore what it means to the people using it. And what happens when they use it in various ways.

Social constructionist approaches can be traced back to the pragmatic philosophy of CS Peirce and John Dewey, coming forward via the work of maverick Soviet educationalist Lev Vygotsky (1978) and linguistic philosophers including Ludwig Wittgenstein and Mikhail Bakhtin to modern writers including Ken Gergen (see for example Gergen, 1999).

This view leads away from the attempted objectivity of positivist science (as perhaps illustrated by the discussion of positive psychology above), and instead points towards the idea of knowledge being constructed locally and publicly in specific contexts by interactions. Meaning is not seen as stable, but shifts across different contexts.

It is therefore not sensible to attempt to measure 'happiness', for example, as if it were a stable 'thing', but instead to look at how the word is used and connected to the contexts which we are seeking to influence. People use the word in different ways and to different ends. Take these two quotations:

> Happiness lies in the joy of achievement and the thrill of creative effort.
> *Franklin D Roosevelt*

> Happiness is nothing more than good health and a bad memory.
> *Albert Schweitzer*

Two people using the same word at different times and in different ways. Rather than look for some kind of 'real' meaning behind the word, social construction looks instead at how the word is *used* in these different ways, and how it relates to, and was helpful in, these different settings.

Both Solutions Focus and Appreciative Inquiry share this fluid philosophy. However, they have developed from different endeavours and in different contexts, which leads to some interesting and subtle differences in emphasis and practice.

Appreciative Inquiry

Appreciative Inquiry (Ai) can be traced back to work by David Cooperider and Suresh Srivastva in 1980. Having been invited to contribute to an analysis of 'what's wrong with with the human side of this organisation', Cooperider was amazed at the level of positive cooperation, innovation and egalitarian governance he saw. Over the years, he, Srivastva and others have developed their ideas into a way of working with organisations.

Organisations, Cooperrider and Srivastva argue, are not 'problems to be solved' but are centres of infinite human capacity – ultimately unpredictable, unknowable, or, a 'mystery alive'. They offer the hypothesis that human systems grow in the direction of what people study – therefore, search for the true, the good, the better and the possible in human systems.

Ai has been defined by Cooperider and Diana Whitney (2004) in these terms:

> Appreciative Inquiry is about the coevolutionary search for the best in people, their organizations, and the relevant world around them. In its broadest focus, it involves systematic discovery of what gives 'life' to a living system when it is most alive, most effective, and most constructively capable in economic, ecological, and human terms. AI involves, in a central way, the art and practice of asking questions that strengthen a system's capacity to apprehend, anticipate, and heighten positive potential.

In practical terms Ai is usually presented as having four distinct stages – the 4-Ds model:

Figure 1

There is now a large Ai community around the world, with many books and resources available (for an introduction, I recommend *The Thin Book to Appreciative Inquiry* (Hammond, 1998) or *Appreciative Inquiry: Change at the Speed of Imagination* (Watkins and Mohr, 2001)). Ai has often been used to take on large-scale organisational challenges, with the deliberate involvement of large numbers of people in interviewing and building change, though this emphasis is shifting to include work with teams, individuals and leaders.

Solutions Focus

While Appreciative Inquiry has its roots in large-scale interventions, Solutions Focus comes from a more intimate setting. Solution Focused Brief Therapy was created by Steve de Shazer and Insoo Kim Berg of the Brief Family Therapy Center, Milwaukee in the late 1970s (see for example de Shazer (1988) and Berg and de Jong (2001)). This discipline was itself based on Gregory Bateson and Milton Erickson's ideas on systems and language, and de Shazer and Berg had studied with members of Bateson's team at the Mental Research Centre in Palo Alto.

Bateson was involved in the early stages of NLP – in the early 1970s it was he who originally suggested to Richard Bandler and John Grinder that they investigate the difference between an excellent performer and an average one, setting in train the process of observation and modelling that has become NLP. NLP is now widely used in organisational work – indeed, the training has become something of a rite of passage in some circles. Solutions Focus, though sharing some common ancient roots, has developed along very different lines.

Seen by some as the ultimate in minimalism and pragmatism, the approach seeks to 'find what works and do more of it' as simply as possible. Great care is taken to follow the philosophical principle of Occam's Razor, resist introducing unnecessary concepts and ideas and look at each case afresh. At the most fundamental level, there are three principles to Solutions Focus working:

1. **Don't fix what isn't broken** – a caution to be quite sure about who wants something to be different and is prepared to do something about it.
2. **Find what works and do more of it** – even in the most difficult situations, there are times when things are better or less bad than usual. How come?
3. **Stop doing what doesn't work and do something different** – on the rare occasions that nothing seems to be working at all.

The order of these principles is important – the initial search is for what is working, in preference to what is not. There are a number of different tools, processes and questions which are used to probe and build ideas about what works – you will find many of them used in this book.

This method has been used with much success in fields such as therapy, schools, child protection and addiction counselling since the 1980s. More recently, it has begun to be applied to organisational issues and is finding a firm foothold amongst people professionals looking for a highly effective, respectful and incisive way of working with leaders, managers, teams and organisations. The Solutions Focus book by Paul Z Jackson and myself has been a rallying point for the many people around the world using the approach.

Solutions Focus (SF), with its roots in therapeutic work, has seen organisational applications in coaching, performance appraisal, teams and strategic planning amongst others. The initial focus on one-to-one and small groups is increasingly being supplemented by larger scale efforts. In this way Ai and SF can be seen as two traditions working alongside each other, with similarities and differences to be enjoyed and utilised.

An interesting comparison between Solutions Focus (SF) and Appreciative Inquiry has been produced (Rossi, Lustig and McKergow, 2003). This shows some interesting similarities and differences, particularly in the kind of words used by both traditions to describe what they do – Ai uses terms like *systematic discovery of what gives 'life' to a living system when it is most alive*, while the minimal SF favours *find what works and do more of it*. These seem to appeal to different people in different ways.

Finally, it seems that positive approaches – of all types and traditions – are coming to the forefront of organisational work. There seems to be much to learn, and much to be learned from all of these different methods. You have already started to join in by reading this far.

References

Buckingham, Marcus and Clifton, Donald O (2002), *Now, Discover Your Strengths*, Free Press.

Berg, Insoo Kim and De Jong, Peter (2001), *Interviewing for Solutions (2nd edition)*, Wadsworth.

Cooperider, David and Whitney, Diana (2004), *What is Appreciative Inquiry?*, AI Commons website, http://appreciativeinquiry.cwru.edu/uploads/whatisai.pdf.

De Shazer, Steve (1988), *Clues: Investigating Solutions in Brief Therapy*, WW Norton.

Gergen, Kenneth J (1999), *An invitation to Social Construction*, SAGE Publications.

Hammond, Sue Annis (1998) *The Thin Book of Appreciative Inquiry*, Thin Book Publishing.

ITS NLP Coaching Certification page, http://www.itsnlp.com/training/coach1.htm, December 2004.

Jackson, Paul Z and McKergow, Mark (2002), *The Solutions Focus: The SIMPLE Way to Positive Change*, London, Nicholas Brealey Publishing.

Rossi, Kendy, Lustig, Tricia and McKergow, Mark (2003), 'A comparison of Appreciative Inquiry (AI) and Solutions Focus (SF)', Appreciative Inquiry Commons website, http://appreciativeinquiry.cwru.edu/research/bibPapersDetail.cfm?coid=3231.

Schein, Edgar H (1988), *Process Consultation Volume 1: Its Role in Organization Development*, Addison-Wesley.

Seligman, Martin (2003), *Authentic Happiness*, London, Nicholas Brealey Publishing.

Seligman, Martin (1998), *Learned Optimism*, Pocket Books.

Vygotsky, Lev S (1978), *Mind in society The development of higher psychological process*, Cambridge, MA, Harvard University Press.

Watkins, Jane McGruder and Mohr, Bernard J (2001) *Appreciative Inquiry: Change at the Speed of Imagination*, Jossey Bass Wiley.

Biographical note

Mark McKergow PhD MBA enjoys doing more with less and keeping things as simple as possible but no simpler. He has consulted and developed people in a wide range of organisations, written over 30 articles and book reviews, is a regular conference speaker in Europe and the USA and has delivered programmes in Solutions Focus around the world. He is co-author, with Paul Z Jackson, of *The Solutions Focus: The SIMPLE Way to Positive Change*. Contact him by email at mark@mckergow.com, or

via www.thesolutionsfocus.com or www.mckergow.com.

Dancing the Solution Focused Shuffle!

Louis Cauffman

What is a Solutions Focused approach? What aspects make it distinctive? Veteran consultant and facilitator Louis Cauffman draws on his long experience with this rigorous tradition and pulls out some key points. It's much more than just acting positively ...

The business world all too often craves for off-the-shelf ways of doing things and for standardised methods and interventions to solve particular problems. However, in our work in the business environment, we have discovered that directly offering solutions to our clients tends not to work too well! Nor does strict adherence to methods or models. The Solutions Focused approach to consulting and coaching (two sides of the same coin, we think) is in essence geared towards flexibility and usefulness. Instead of making suggestions and giving advice, we ask questions, special questions: solution-building questions. Instead of rigidly following a model, our aim is to be flexible – and as useful as we can to the client.

In our Solutions Focused Coachulting practice, we have developed an eight-step dance. We have also collected solutions-building questions to deploy during the dance. As you read this article, we invite you to dance along. Would it be useful to let your own business case play in your mind while reading this article? Would it be interesting to jot down some ideas about what you might use in the interaction with your client, after reading this article?

The eight-step dance of Solutions Focused coaching

What follows are the different steps of the Solution Focused 'dance'. You can combine these steps into an idiosyncratic combination that suits the specific situation you are dealing with as a Solution Focused coach/consultant. The process-protocol that is embedded in the eight-step dance is an orderly, ever changing way of co-operating with our clients that is geared towards solutions. Yet, when one uses the eight-step dance, you will discover that the steps are not taken randomly! Dancing the Solution Focused shuffle looks more like a tango than like hopping around in an unorganised way.

1.   Socialising

The motor of change is the working relationship between the coach and his client (system). Taking care of a positive and co-operative working relationship not only allows you to get away with mistakes but also boosts progress. Socialising is always the very first step one takes when meeting a client. You shake hands, ask if the client could find your office easily, ask 'How is business?' etc. Socialising goes from small talk to showing your interest in whatever interests the client.

2.   Clarifying the context

Nobody works in a vacuum; no business operates in a vacuum. We always have to take into account the context in which the problem occurs. Otherwise you will fall into a 'simplistic solutionism', a solution orientation of the flattest kind. Problem: 'Doctor, if I touch this it hurts. What should I do?' Solution: 'Stop touching it.' Later, the patient dies of a cancer that could have been cured if it had been detected quickly. Examining a problem without considering its context minimises the possibility of finding a real solution. Moreover, asking questions about the context shows the client that we are more interested in them as person or company than solely in their problems.

CASE:
Two large banks were planning to merge. A task force was set up to guide the process. The chairman of the work group was well aware of the fact that competition could arise between the employees of the merging partners. By first asking everyone which elements of their previous company they definitely wanted to keep, he gave them the opportunity to make concrete propositions. Then, taking these propositions into account, he offered a consensus about the task force's goals. From this he deduced that a slogan – 'the best of both' – could serve as a guideline for further development of the process. Thus, when tension arose during the course of the merger, the project manager could fall back on this created context. This made it easier for everyone involved to avoid the traps these types of processes often fall into. It also helped both banks to quickly gear their procedures – both internal and external – toward each other.

3. Goal setting

The art of Solution Focused Coaching lies in the reshaping and redefining of the goals towards do-able and useful goals that then become beacons on the road to success. How to do this? By asking solution-building questions.

Finding clear, concrete and realistic goals that are important to the client and his company, leads the coaching intervention to swift and lasting results. The question: 'What should we discuss in this meeting to make this conversation useful?' is the standard question to initiate goal setting. You can use this question when starting every meeting in order to get focused on goals and avoid talking hot air.

The 5 characteristics of useful goals are:
1. Realistic
2. Realisable
3. Pragmatic
4. Defined in terms of observable behaviour
5. Preferably from small to big

4. Exceptions

There isn't a single problem in the world that is there all the time and with the same intensity. Solution Focused coaches focus on these exception times since they are partial solutions. Elaborating these partial solutions by using solution-building questions promotes gradual change towards more permanent solutions. The Solution Focused coach concentrates on the 'who, how, what, when, and where' of exceptions.

CASE:

Janet complains that her co-workers consistently ignore her during team meetings and is so irritated by this that she is at odds with her team colleagues. The Solution Focused coach will not suggest that she try talking to her co-workers about the problem. (Janet's answer to this suggestion would most likely be: 'I have already tried that many times and it only makes things worse.') It is better to look for the moments in which she *does* have positive contact with her colleagues. We call these moments 'exceptions to the problem'. If it turns out that her colleagues don't ignore her during small, informal meetings, the Solution Focused coach will ask her to further investigate these moments: How do you react to your colleagues during these informal meetings when the conversation is going well? How do you behave differently then? What exactly do you say then? The next step is to help her to translate that behaviour into the team meeting setting.

5. Hunting for resources

Traditional models assume that problems arise because of a staff member's deficiency or inability to create a solution. The solution-building approach holds the assumption that the employees involved in the problem *do* have the resources to solve that problem. The job of the solution-building manager is to help the employees to (re)discover these 'forgotten' resources and/or to give them new tools to build solutions. In this context, we define 'resources' as every available tool that can be used to create solutions. Resources can be things as intangible as effort, motivation, loyalty to the company, collegiality, or expertise, but they also can be more concrete tools, such as communication skills, crisis and conflict management, procedures, business insights, technical tools, time, money or attention. Sometimes what initially seems negative can be considered a positive: a crisis can become an opportunity, a setback in business opens your eyes, loss of clients prompt you to pay more attention to clients, complaints may encourage you to be more customer-oriented, your company's weaknesses may become opportunities for improvement, threats become chances – the list goes on.

6. Giving compliments

Compliment giving is an important skill that is seriously neglected. For solution-building managers, giving compliments is a natural way of communicating with people. They don't give compliments just to be friendly or to garner approval from their colleagues. The point of giving compliments is to build a positive working relationship, give the client self-confidence, elicit a solution focus instead of a problem focus, and support and increase the likelihood of change. Compliments are a powerful confirmation of the useful behaviour of employees. And try to remember: 'Every compliment yields a dividend!'

7. Offering differentiation

People often think in absolute terms: they feel good or they feel bad. Something goes well or goes poorly. The company results are good or bad. The light is on or off. It's black or white. But most matters in life, and in business, aren't black and white – the range of greys is almost infinite. (There are only a few exceptions: you are dead or alive, pregnant or not.) In fact, such black-and-white thinking will quickly trap us into believing that a problem isn't really solved until everything is perfect, while in reality, small improvement is often the first step toward a solution.

The solution-building model uses a ten-point scale to help to reveal these shades of grey. The 'Scale of Progress' is great technique to both elicit change and to measure progress toward a solution. It can be asked in the following way: 'If I were to ask you to situate yourself somewhere on a scale from 0 to 10, where 0 indicates the moment when you were performing badly on the job and 10 indicates the moment when you think the problems have been sufficiently solved to continue working comfortably and functionally, where would you say you are at this moment?' Accept whatever number your employee mentions and then ask: ' OK, so you say you are on a 3. Good; now what is already happening so that you are able to give it a 3?' Help the employee to elaborate the answer in as much detail as possible. Make abundant use of the question 'What else?' as this will help to elicit more lively details and keep your employee going. Continue this line of questioning by asking: 'What is the smallest next step that could move you up on the scale? What would it take?'

8.   Future orientation

Problems by definition belong to the past while solutions by definition belong to the future. The Solution Focused coach/consultant helps his clients to face away from the problem and look at possible solutions. A great technique to do this, the Miracle Question, was invented by Steve de Shazer. Solution-building managers introduce the miracle question by asking clients if they will grant them permission to ask a peculiar question that initially may seem irrelevant. After the client has given the manager permission, he or she asks the following question (preferably in a slightly dramatised way):

Imagine that you go to sleep tonight, and while you are sleeping a miracle happens. And in that miracle, all the problems you are dealing with now, are solved just enough so that they do not bother you so much any more. But you do not know that since you were sleeping! You wake up not knowing that the miracle has occurred. How would you know a miracle has happened? What would you do differently? What would make you realise the miracle had happened?

The miracle question is useful for several reasons. First, the word 'miracle' gives the client permission to think about the widest spectrum of possibilities. After all, a miracle doesn't have any boundaries or rules. Therefore, the client is prompted to think broadly. Second, the question circumvents resistance: because the answer need not be part of the 'rational' world, there is no need to use rational counter-arguments. Third, the miracle question is future-oriented – the answers are connected to a future in which problems are no longer problems. The miracle question de-emphasises the problems of today and yesterday and refocuses the client's attention toward a possible future in which more satisfactory solutions are at hand. Fourth, it is an elegant way to elicit clear, future-oriented objectives from clients. Finding solutions becomes much easier once clear objectives have been set.

Solution-building questions

Of course, the 'dance' is conducted by way of conversation. Asking questions is a more collaborative way of having a conversation than constantly taking the lead. Questions are midwives for solutions – they shape the answers you get. Asking the right questions helps you to set the correct tone and build further solutions. People usually ask questions to elicit information. However, Solution Focused coaches go further. They ask questions to help people to evaluate their own perspective on the problems and to direct the conversation toward solutions. When you follow up on the answers with even more solution-building questions, you will notice that you are building solutions together.

The following list contains some basic solution-building questions that you can alter and build upon in your own ways.

- What should we discuss in this meeting to make sure that the time is usefully spent? (Goal setting)
- How will you know that the problem is solved? How will you notice this? What would you do differently then? (Future orientation)

- What would be the smallest step you could take to solve this problem? (Differentiation: making big goals more workable)
- How would the other departments notice that you are making progress? What would your boss say you would be doing differently if things improved? (Differentiation: expanding the possible solutions into the system)
- What else do you have to tell me so that I can see this situation even more clearly? (Clarifying the context: eliciting co-operation from the client)
- Have you ever solved similar problems? How did you solve them on that occasion? Who helped you? How did he or she help you? (Exceptions and hunting for resources)
- Are there moments in which the problem is less intense? What is different then? (Exceptions and differentiation)
- Has anything changed since you scheduled this meeting about the conflicts concerning the project? (Clarifying; exceptions; differentiation: eliciting signs of spontaneous 'pre-session' changes)
- Now that you have achieved that, what is the next small step you could take? (Future orientation: success builds/breeds on success)
- Imagine that this problem is solved. What will be different then? What will you do differently? What will your colleagues do differently? What will the management do differently? (Future orientation; differentiation)

Dancing the shuffle

The owner of a carpet manufacturing company had experienced some health problems and consequently had been absent frequently during the past two years. Once recovered and working again full time, he began colliding with his son-in-law. He was convinced that his son-in-law had seized the opportunity to take charge of the company. The son-in-law believed that it was his duty to keep the business running and that he had therefore earned the right to continue managing the company in the same way he had during the owner's absence. The conflict also affected the family. The daughter was caught in the middle and the mother was blamed for choosing sides whenever she tried to get them to reconcile. This negative atmosphere extended even to the shop floor: the personnel received contradictory orders and had the feeling that they were being used as pawns.

How should the situation be approached? To aim to stop the misunderstandings and arguments would be to run the risk of getting involved in the tangle of conflicts. Both men would try to convince you that he is right or, even worse, would force you to choose a side – a type of 'if you're not on my side you're against me' thinking. It is better to ask questions that help both men to think about co-operating again.

Each was asked separately: 'What has to change to regain order and peace?' (*Goal setting; future orientation*). The father-in-law's first answer was: 'My son-in-law has to stop shutting me out.' The son-in-law said: 'My father-in-law has to stop interfering with my work and leave me alone.' These answers were not very useful. To the question 'What could and would you do differently to make things easier?' (*Goal setting*) the father-in-law answered: 'We can't go on the way we are acting now. I will try to be friendly to him but I'm not going to butter him up.' The son-in-law said: 'I could ask my father-in-law to join the meetings I've organised with my production team, but he shouldn't snap at me during the meeting.' With these answers, both of them gave a little opening to something useful.

Our next question was: 'What is the smallest sign that will show you that things are going better?' (*Differentiation*). The son-in-law replied: 'I would feel more at ease and I wouldn't be on edge when my father-in-law is around.' The father-in-law answered: 'My son-in-law wouldn't avoid me anymore.' We followed this with: 'What would you do differently when you notice that you are more at ease when your father-in-law is around?' and: 'What would you do differently if you were to notice that your son-in-law is no longer avoiding you?' (*Differentiation*). The answers to these questions help them paint a detailed picture of possible solutions.

As the conversation progressed both men were more willing to change their attitudes toward each other. The father-in-law agreed to try to act positively toward his son-in-law. He translated this into being more friendly, inviting him for a drink on Sunday, agreeing with him in the presence of their co-workers (or remaining silent if he didn't agree), and trying to find it in his heart to say something positive when his son-in-law did something well. The son-in-law planned to inform his father-in-law weekly about the state of affairs of production, to go through the orders with him, to present the quality-control figures, and to show interest in his proposals.

Conclusion

Combining solution talk and solution-building questions while dancing along the eight-step dance allows you to maximise your efficiency as Solution Focused coach/consultant. Have fun!

Biographical note
Louis Cauffman is Director-Owner of the Korzybski Foundation (www.korzybski.com), an international training institute in Solution Focused Brief Therapy with branches in Belgium, Holland and France. His is also Director-Owner of the Integrative Management Institute bvba, a consulting company that specialises both in family-owned business AND in Solution Focused Board Room Coaching & Strategic Management for (multi)national (not-for) profit companies.

For more articles that you can freely download, visit: www.solution-focused-management.com

Address:
Louis Cauffman
Marcel Habetslaan 31
b-3600 GENK BELGIUM
+32 89 38 33 22

Originally published in Organisations and People, Volume 10, Number 4, pages 6–11.

Appreciative Inquiry:

Social Construction in Practice

Sheila McNamee

Appreciative inquiry offers us a resource for coordinating multiple values, beliefs, and activities. As an illustration of social construction in action, it is one approach that invites us to create new organisational realities together.

Many of the traditional and trusted understandings of organisational theory and practice have come under sharp question as our organisations become globalised. Theorists, researchers, and organisational leaders are all recognising that organisational life is part of everyone's life. Organisations are central players in shaping the economy, the political agenda, the physical environment, as well as the sense of community – both locally and globally. Organisational life is deeply intertwined with issues of central importance to us such as how we educate our children, how we integrate diversity into our lives, how we generate a sense of what is valued, and how we rebuild neglected countries, cities, and neighbourhoods. Organisational life is about *sustainable life forms*. It is an area of study where we come to understand how our actions create the worlds in which we live.

This said, we must accept that the quality of future life on the globe depends on the outcome of newly emerging forms of organisational process. Based on an understanding that the most pressing issues of our time transcend organisational, cultural, and even national boundaries, organisational leaders are experimenting with new cooperative ways of doing business in which the dialogic construction of values, beliefs, knowledge, ethics, and daily practice generate sustainable results. This interest places communication at the forefront of organisational understanding.

How can our forms of practice engender collaborative partner-ships where diverse voices, competing ideologies, and opposing traditions can all be heard and respected? Is it possible, we must ask, to abandon our desire to 'discover' *the* proper way of making deci-sions, putting plans to action, mediating conflict, and so forth? Can we, instead, examine organisational practices from an orientation of 'interested inquiry' where we explore how various and often competing discursive traditions enable possibilities? Can we do this without requiring consensus, which attempts to erase differences, and instead strive toward transformative dialogue where multiplic-ity is coordinated rather than obliterated? Social construction offers us just this opportunity.

Social construction

The relational orientation of social construction requires that we replace our emphasis on individuals and their internal motivations, intentions and perceptions with an emphasis, instead, on the coor-dinated activities of people engaging with one another. We want to focus on people *conversing* with one another, where *conversation* is used in the most general sense encompassing all forms of bodily and verbal engagement.

For the social constructionist, then, communication does not require competent or accurate conveyance of one's meanings to another. Rather, meaning is created in the coordination of activities among people. To that end, meaning is *actively* coordinated by *us* in our on going activities. As you converse with others, the meaning of your words and actions has the potential to change, shift, and alter. Meaning is never fixed. It is not stable and unchanging. There is, then, no way for me, once and for all, to tell you what I 'mean'.

Appreciative inquiry offers us one resource for coordinating multiple values, beliefs, and activities. As an illustration of social construction in action, it is one approach that invites us to create new organisational realities together – organisational realities that allow participants to *go on together*, in Wittgenstein's (1953) words. By exploring the potentials for relational forms of practice, as I believe appreciative inquiry does, we can add rich and supple resources to our repertoire of extant practices. The main point of all this work, to me, is to recognise that forms of practice are options not truths.

Resources for relational practice

When we are confronted with diverse commitments and beliefs, when we are faulted for our actions or tempted to fault others for theirs, we can use the reservoir of other voices to move conversation beyond conflict, blame, dysfunction, or inadequacy toward collaborative coordination. We can explore actions within some relational configuration rather than *as self contained individuals* (Sampson, 1993).

My colleague, Kenneth Gergen, and I have suggested four particular relational resources: internal others, conjoint relations, relations among groups, and the systemic swim (1998). Each of these resources draws upon a dimension of our relational being. And, as I illustrate, each offers an opening for not only new resources for action but for novel ways to invite others into constructing generative organisational practices.

Internal others

We all carry with us many voices, many differing opinions, views and attitudes – even on the same subject. These voices represent the accumulation of our past relationships. In effect, we carry the residues of many others with us; 'we contain multitudes'. Yet, most of our actions – along with the positions we adopt in conversations

– are one dimensional. Communication becomes quickly patterned, regardless of the many resources we have for transforming our problematic conversations. What we actually do in unwanted but repeated patterns is represent only a small segment of all that we might do and say. In cases where we are prompted to blame individuals, we might ask: 'What other voices are available to this person, and to me? How can they be brought into the conversation?'

It is here that appreciative inquiry becomes a practical application of social constructionist principles. As Cooperrider (1990, 1995) articulates, most of our talk in organisations is based on the premise that 'organising is a problem to be solved'. Thus, we engage in 'problem solving talk' which requires us to define the problem, analyse what the causes of the problem are, explore why attempted solutions have failed and work to develop an action plan.

If the reality we live is constructed by what we do with others, then when we are talking about and relating with each other around problems, we are constructing a reality of problems. Cooperrider's suggestion is that we begin instead with the premise that *organising is a mystery to be embraced*. Starting here invites us into conversations about what we value, about our 'high points', and our dreams. When we invite each other into conversations focused on past, present, and future possibilities and successes, our entire set of options shift. We find ourselves engaged in the construction of potential.

The literature on appreciative inquiry is abundant with illustrations of just this sort of practice. Researchers and consultants alike have found generative ways to invite organisational members to communicate with their voice of appreciation rather than their voice of fault-finding which, unfortunately, is the typical one invited into organisational life (see for example, Barrett (1995), and Hammond and Royal (1998) to name only two excellent sources).

Conjoint relations

Now our focus shifts to the domain of public interchange or joint action. We are not concerned with action–reaction cycles but with patterns where each action depends on another for its intelligibility. Focus is on the way in which meanings are generated, sustained and disrupted in relationships.

Actions, in themselves, have no meaning. There is no means of extricating self from other. One's actions are never independent. They acquire intelligibility as actions by virtue of others. Again, we can note how appreciative inquiry, when coupled with this notion of conjoint relations, can shift organisational practices beyond impasse and conflict. Unlike my earlier suggestion to call upon the 'voice of appreciation' in self or the other, here our focus might be on valuing how *we* achieve or even do not achieve certain potentials in our organisational life.

Can we centre our attention on the magic of our *joint achievements* thereby demonising no one person? Might we capitalise on how we can move toward preferred futures *together*? One effective way to denaturalise our unproductive but ritualised practices in organisations is to talk about these patterns as *cooperative constructions* rather than accomplishments of one individual.

Relations among groups

We often use the language of individualism to refer to, or describe, the operations of larger groups. For example, we say, 'the organisation decided', or 'government controls', or 'the family feels'. We similarly use this language to talk about relations among groups: 'business beliefs about government', or 'the Smith family's anger at the Joneses'. Even disciplinary talk takes this form: political scientists describe nations as struggling or competing, sociologists describe the ambitions of social movements, communication scholars refer to the symmetry of relationships.

By transforming individualist talk to broader social groups we move rituals of individual blame into the relational sphere. We now see the individual's actions as manifestations of larger aggregates.

For example, a husband's unprovoked anger is seen as a manifestation of competition in the workplace. Theft becomes an issue of economic class relations. Individuals only serve as exemplars of relationships among groups. Further, we are compelled to understand our construction of another's actions in terms of the larger institutions by which we are constituted. What we define as theft we do by virtue of our privileged place in the class structure. Yet, within the framework of those engaged in the action, it is seen as heroism or self-preservation.

We find that appreciative inquiry, combined with this relational focus, illustrates the powerful potential of social constructionist practice in organisations. By focusing on the significant groups or communities with which members from an organisation affiliate, and by using the discourse of appreciation, we draw ourselves and others into conversations that are marked by what I call *interested inquiry*. That is, we become *curious* about unseen communities and groups that might support or value the actions of an organisational member.

It is important to note here that appreciating and valuing relations among groups is not introducing irrelevant information into our organisational operations. In the global economy of today, the number of communities and groups that any one person affiliates with is expansive. To silence these voices in our organisational life is akin to allowing only a fraction of each person into the organisation. To the extent that we make these other communities irrelevant to our organisational activities, we impede our ability to coordinate the complexities of social life and thus we construct our organisations as *artificial communities* that are dissociated from the wide range of relations we engage.

Systemic process

In many fields – ecology, physics, mysticism, spirituality – there is a presumption that the universe is not comprised of isolated units. If any unit can be related to any other, the landscape of possibilities for understanding any action is without horizon. How are our problems as an organisation related to our family relationships, the state of the economy, increasing crime rates, depletion of the ozone? Can we ask, 'How is this action reflecting the context in which this individual works, the state of our relationship at this point, the condition of the country and other events or conditions that might be relevant?'

The idea of systemic process combined with organisational inquiry that is premised on the discourse of appreciation is illustrative of social construction in action. When organisational members act they are not *telling the truth* or *operating from universal, objective principles.* They are, instead, *inviting* others into particular forms of organisational life. And, if my actions are not seen as *representing* the ways things *should* be, but rather as manifestations of myriad social processes, might we begin to value the variation? Might we begin to take note of the ways in which diversity contributes positively to organisational life? Might we begin to *expect* differences rather than assign difference the status of 'problem' in the organisation?

Again we see that with this approach our organisations will coordinate multiplicity rather than suppress it. To me, this is a prerequisite for organisational life in today's global economy.

Elements of the appreciative organisation

There are several organisational practices that emerge from the above discussion. In what follows, I will focus attention on one common aspect of organisational life: evaluation or the review process. Let us consider how relationally oriented practices, generated within the discourse of appreciation and value might refigure evaluation in organisations.

Focus on relational configurations, not individuals

Relationships are the primary source of good and bad, right and wrong. Traditional review or evaluation processes in organisations are attempts to give feedback to members about their 'fit' with what is 'right or good' for the organisation. In the appreciative organisation, the expectation is that different segments of the organisation are likely to have translated organisational values into different forms of practice. If leadership is valued in one segment, team work might well be valued in another. These differences are not seen as competing but rather as coherent forms of practice and sense-making that emerge from the day-to-day activities of members. The chore of adjudicating which set of values and priorities is 'right' gives way to the creativity of crafting opportunities where these different realities can be engaged. In place of the stability and uniformity of the traditional organisation, the appreciative organisation finds ways of valuing diversity.

Include multiple voices

Organisations are populated by many and diverse members. The inclusion of all voices provides the opportunity for the many nuances members contribute to the overall effectiveness of the organisation. The appreciative organisation creates opportunities for members not directly aligned to come together. Introducing members from distinctly different segments of the organisation, who might not otherwise or ordinarily need to know each other or know about each other's work, could potentially improve organisational functioning. When it comes to the process of review, valuing these various voices contributes to the overall sense of an appreciative organisation.

Generate participatory practices

To shift from evaluation to valuation in organisations requires inviting all members into the process of review. Standards set by a few relay a message that only those few members are experienced enough to judge the performance of others. Generating participatory practices, particularly in the process of review or in creating the terms for review, allows members to coordinate their various views about effective and productive contributions for the organisation.

Envision effective futures

Where traditional evaluation focuses on one's past performance, the appreciative organisation focuses on valuing what might be possible for the future. Organisational members are likely to become inspired and hopeful as they collaborate with colleagues on how to further move the organisation forward. The excitement of members' visions for the future ignites creativity in constructing action plans. If colleagues know where another's abilities and interests are focused, the group can work together to enhance possibilities for further development and use of those interests and talents. The entire organisation benefits.

Emphasise and coordinate strengths, abilities, and passions

In the appreciative organisation, the focus is on members' interdependencies, on the potential for new meanings to emerge in the fostering of new connections, on respect and caring of all relationship potentials, on dialogue, possibilities, continuous conversation, and stories of success and appreciation. These features leave little room for the tradition of evaluation where dialogue centres on what is not working well. In the appreciative organisation, one member's success is every member's success and is catalytic in the continual evolution of the organisation.

How might organisations be different if the voice of appreciation and possibility were dominant?

In my own context, a university, I attempt to engage in relational forms of practice such as appreciative inquiry. As a professor I see the classes I teach, the committees on which I serve, and my general orientation to the organisation we call 'the university', as 'laboratories' for putting into practice my more theoretical and conceptual writings on the relational construction of realities. All of these contexts, as well as my professional work outside the university help me to reflect on the potentials of relational practice and the myriad ways in which to engage relationally.

In my own organisational context the difficulty comes when I confront the dominant organisational tradition of the university itself. Then, I need to constantly remind myself that change in small arenas is significant change and probably the most useful place to begin. Just a few of the changes I have noticed in my own use of relational practices are:

- Taking time, sometimes what seems like an enormous amount of time, in the beginning of a class, project, or implementation of a new programme to develop relationships where all members feel their differences are respected on their own terms. This reduces 'work time' later on for the group. By finding a way to locate each other's orientation to a given topic, task, project within a set of relationships that are *significant* for each person, we move closer to finding a way to coordinate multiple discourses rather than strive for consensus where no one is really satisfied. I have found this extremely useful in moving to an appreciation for diversity.
- Defining together what will count as 'success' or 'improvement', for example, helps to create a relational context where people can coordinate their multiplicity. Again, these interpretations can only be crafted cooperatively if we *begin* with an appreciation for differences as well as an assumption of actions as coherent and valued in *some* community or group.
- Moving from discussing abstract principles to creating an atmosphere of participation. Stories help us to achieve this goal. While I can disagree with your position on a principle, I can not tell you that the story of your experience is wrong. If we invite others to tell us their stories – and more importantly, if we ask them to tell stories of high points, successes, excitement within the organisation – we are more likely to become intrigued, curious, inquisitive, and engaged. In our curiosity and engagement come possibilities for relational engagement of a different genre; one based on value and recognition among organisational members.

- By recognising our own part in constructing situations, we can engage differently where we tend to disagree by valuing curiosity and relationships rather than by simply trying to eliminate those actions, persons, or issues.

These are only a few of the possibilities that open when we invite alternative constructions of organisational life.

At this point, it is useful to note that within the constructionist discourse, theory itself is a form of coordinated activity. This is important because we generally give theory the power of description, explanation, and prediction. If our theories can 'get it right' about the social world we need only refer to those theories to know how to act in the world with success. If theory is granted this superior status, then epistemology is boxed within a world where one either has or does not have an epistemology that 'gets it right'.

However, within a constructionist realm, any particular theory serves as a *discourse* for action. A theory invites particular forms of practice and eliminates others. The interesting question to ask is not whether a particular theoretical stance is true or not but what a particular stance allows us to do together and what it prohibits. To provide a constructionist summary of the issue, theory is not taken as a 'truth telling' but is recognised as a form of coordinated activity among persons. Thus, theory becomes practical or generative (Gergen, 1994).

Some closing thoughts

What does this relational view of organisational life allow us to do, where joint action is taken as the source of knowledge? With this emphasis we become curious about the conversations that create the problems, the successes, and the realities lived in organisations. We face the challenge of fostering organisational environments that invite us to focus on what people do together. We must consider how to give voice to the multiple discourses present and to the movement of conversations in and around our organisations. This is what gives life to an organisation.

Perhaps a focus on the discourse of appreciation, of value, of what works and of dreams could effectively replace our attention on individual characteristics that are assumed to 'make' the organisation succeed. The focus of organising in a global world is on changing conversations, not changing people.

References

Barrett, FJ (1995), 'Creating Appreciative Learning Cultures', *Organisational Dynamics*, vol. 24, no. 1, pp. 36–49.

Cooperrider DL (1990), 'Positive Image, Positive Action: The Affirmative Basis of Organizing', in S Srivastva and DL Cooperrider (eds), *Appreciative Management and Leadership: The Power of Positive Thought and Action in Organizations*, San Francisco, CA, Jossey-Bass Inc.

Cooperrider, DL (1995), 'Introduction to Appreciative Inquiry', in W French and C Bell (eds), *Organisation Development* (5th ed.), New York, Prentice Hall.

Gergen KJ (1992), *The Saturated Self*, New York, Basic Books.

Hammond, S and Royal, C (eds) (1998), *Lessons from the Field: Applying Appreciative Inquiry*, Plano, TX, Practical Press, Inc.

McNamee, S and Gergen, KJ (1998), *Relational Responsibility: Resources for Sustainable Dialogue*, Thousand Oaks, California, Sage.

Sampson, EE (1993), *Celebrating the Other*, Colorado, Westview Press.

Wittgenstein, L (1953), *Philosophical Investigations*, trans. G Anscombe, New York, Macmillan.

Biographical note

Doctor Sheila McNamee is Professor of Communication at the University of New Hampshire. She has written extensively on social constructionist theory and practice. In her work, she brings together many different communities with diametrically opposing viewpoints to create liveable futures. She can be contacted at: sheila.mcnamee@unh.edu.

Originally published in Organisations and People, Volume 9, Number 2, pages 35–41.

Team Remotivation

John Henden

How can a company decimated by mass redundancy pick itself up and carry on? When there are so many financial, interpersonal and emotional problems, how can solution talk find a way in? Is the Solution Focused approach merely a 'sticking plaster' strategy or is it long lasting? John Henden uses a team remotivation process to show one example of the power of SF in organisations.

Background

All organisations go through difficult times, but a Solution Focused approach can bring about better times more quickly.

A successful UK company with a ten-year track record had recently suffered a setback: their main financial backer for a major project withdrew temporarily, due to problems of their own. Although the withdrawal was 'temporary', an interim shutdown period of 9 months, 12 months and even 18 months was discussed. Complete shutdown was avoided as the future contract was very lucrative and the factory and machinery had to be kept in readiness. In the meantime, small short-term contracts could be arranged and some of the office space could be rented out to pay the remaining staff.

The company, understandably, was in shock at first and then, on realising they would not be able to pay all their employees, immediately entered into a redundancy process, laying off 3/5ths of the workforce. After a few more months, another round of redundancies led to the workforce being reduced to 1/7th of its previous size. Of the two dozen or so left, nine were Heads of Department (HoDs).

The factory was like a ghost town, compared with the high level activity and vibrancy at the same time the previous year. Managers and staff could be seen now ambling from department to department, often looking downcast and disinterested, trying to maintain their own personal morale. They found great difficulty, too, trying to keep colleagues motivated.

The company had an added problem. Throughout its growth and right from its early days, whenever a problem or difficulty had arisen, the approach was always to call a meeting to discuss the problem, analyse it, try and discover who was to blame and then decide whose responsibility it was to try and sort it out. These meetings had a history of being lengthy, of discovering other problems and leaving participants sapped of energy and creativity.

The General Manager (GM) realised after a few months into the shutdown phase, that something had to be done. Both managers and staff were showing signs of dispiritedness and hopelessness, feeling bereaved for their former colleagues; and feeling guilty for having survived the double wave of redundancies. The GM wanted to arrest the slide. He called us in to try and remotivate his workforce.

The task

The GM was well versed in how we worked and had had some Solution Focused performance coaching himself. He asked for 'A Remotivation Session' – one workshop for the HoDs and one for the staff. His request was articulated as follows: 'This solution focused stuff is highly regarded. We've got to get the survivors up off the floor and back into harness, to keep them going during the shutdown and actually to produce something during this next year or so. We've got to get them re-motivated and quickly, but you'll have to do it all in two morning sessions because that's all we can afford!'

The workshops

The first workshop for the HoDs was arranged for four weeks following the briefing; and the second, for the remaining staff, occurred two weeks later. Both workshops were conducted along similar lines, although the first, naturally, was given more of a management orientation. Both were held on site: the advantages of this seemed to outweigh, slightly, the disadvantages.

Encouraging an SF orientation from the outset

Being aware of the historical tendency to focus on problems and, knowing the extent of the current negative feelings, I thought it might be helpful to begin by stating broadly how we work. Also, I noticed as attendees were filing in, two in particular seemed to be exhibiting features of clinical depression.

After the initial welcome and introductions and the now customary light-hearted opening, I referred the group to a pre-prepared wall poster thus:

HOW WE WORK

Acknowledgement

        Validation

      Present-future focus

Normalising

              Leapfrogging

Time Quake

      Small Steps

Highlighting strengths, skills & resources

Hope

             Optimism

Solution Building

Figure 1 – How we work

Simply by highlighting these key words, hopes and spirits seemed to rise just a tiny bit at this earliest point. My main objective was to encourage a Solutions Focus (SF) from the outset and this was achieved. (Jackson and McKergow 2002)

Introductions

As part of the introduction process, I outlined previous experience in working with trauma survival: both on a one-to-one basis and with groups. I mentioned both military and civilian contexts and alluded to the most recent critical incident debriefing work, following Foot and Mouth Disease, where a lot of useful work had been done with field officers, veterinary surgeons and slaughterers. It was explained to the group that in many cases, although the contexts are different, the feelings afterwards of loss and guilt about survival were often the same.

After my introduction, I asked each of the group to introduce themselves by name, department and: 'one thing you enjoy doing in your spare time that helps you relax/de-stress'. This last part seemed to have the desired effect of both producing some problem-free talk and to encourage a further SF to the morning's session. The solution-oriented 12 point plan for running workshops (Cameron 1998) is always helpful in getting things off to a good start; and we established some good ground rules.

The group's hopes and expectations

I explained to the group that, whilst I had prepared an outline of what I thought might be helpful and useful to them, this was not cast in stone. I would be most happy to accommodate what they, individually, were wanting and was therefore prepared to make adjustments to meet those needs. From a paired exercise, the most salient hopes and expectations were:

- 'To come away with something positive to say to someone else.'
- 'To feel re-motivated again.'
- 'To get some clarity on what I might achieve during the year's shutdown.'
- 'To get more of a sense of what and how other people are feeling.'

The resultant chart was pinned prominently and I promised I would be glancing at it throughout the session to ensure all elements were met.

Gripes and complaints

In working in a true SF way, I find it is important always to hear the problem out in sufficient (but not too much) detail, in order to move people on. If this is not done adequately, problem talk will keep punctuating the process; people will not have felt heard and they will struggle to adopt an SF mode in their thinking, feelings and actions.

Very clearly, I introduced this part of the session as: 'The Gripes & Complaints Slot', explaining its purpose 'For me to check out that your complaining skills are up to scratch'. By using the term 'slot', I introduced the notion of boundarying; my statement giving it a bit of light-heartedness, whilst not detracting from the seriousness of the task.

This task's 3-fold objective was to:

- Allow sufficient expression of unexpressed thoughts and feelings.
- Get 'the negative stuff' out of the way.
- Promote a sense of re-connectedness within the group.

The power of this exercise was quite amazing. Gradually each participant came forth with their own individual complaints about key individuals, whom they felt they had to name publicly. Many, as they made their contributions, referred to the confidentiality ground rule, and therefore felt safe to express themselves fully. There was much 'Hear, hear' and 'Me, too' and 'Yes, I agree'. Also, there was a little, 'I didn't know you felt that way' and, 'If only I'd known, we could have had a chat', etc. The session lasted for some 25 minutes, but very early on the three objectives were being achieved easily.

Survivors' strengths and resources

Being mindful of Yvonne Dolan's (Dolan 1999) three-stage process of abuse and trauma survival (victimhood, survivorhood and living the authentic life), I thought it useful to examine some aspects of surviving – firstly, the bad news; secondly, the withdrawal of financial backing; and then thirdly, the redundancy process. I was keen, within this section of the workshop, to provide plenty of acknowledgement (Miller, et al. 1996), validation and normalisation around all feelings expressed. This part was introduced by acknowledging that they would have had to deal with a lot personally and would also have found themselves carrying the hurt and disappointment of others. As HoDs, they would have had to make some harsh decisions during the redundancy process, in many cases, involving close colleagues and staff.

Then followed an important SF strategy. I suggested that many of them would have been surprised by the personal strengths, qualities and resources that were brought into play to help them get through this difficult time. There followed a paired exercise for each to tell the other what their particular ones were. During the plenary, all of their declared skills, strengths and resources were flagged up. They were heartened and greatly encouraged that two flip chart sheets were filled and displayed prominently in the room.

I asked which items from this list would be particularly helpful to them, either individually or as a group, to face the next year or so of the shutdown. For some ten minutes or so, participants offered thoughtful suggestions and a degree of discussion ensued about some particular qualities. Each suggestion in turn was highlighted.

Worst case scenario

In my experience in working with these sorts of issues/problems, when things have gone from bad to worse, there is an underlying and often unspoken fear that things could get even worse or lead to total disaster. Such fear can sap energy and maintain 'stuckness' within the problem situation. This exercise then, gets all these ideas out into the open. I explained the purpose of the exercise, something along the lines above, before popping the following question:

'Over the next few weeks and months, what is the worst thing that could happen?'

The following 'worst cases' were amongst the main ones to emerge:

'The main contract won't happen for two years or more'
'There will be even more redundancies amongst us'
'The small contracts we have, won't come to much'
'The office space rentals will produce too little'
'The site here will be sold off and become a housing estate'

Figure 2 – Worst cases

Once we had exhausted ideas of this 'doom & gloom' nature, I moved back swiftly into a solution focus with an exercise called 'Time Quake': I described this as an act of 'leap frogging'.

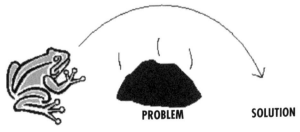

PROBLEM **SOLUTION**

Figure 3 – Leap frogging

Time Quake

The participants next were divided into two groups of six and given the script in Figure 4.

TIME QUAKE

We are going to set up an imaginary meeting like this in (say) 6 months time. Things have improved considerably in the meantime. Our purpose at that meeting is to find out:-

1. What is better?
2. How do we notice things are better?
3. What are you most proud of?
4. Where do you stand on the progress scale?
5. How did you manage to get there?

Figure 4 – Time Quake

The purpose of this exercise was to jet the team into the future, when things were better, and to get a 'video description' of how things will be. Rather like the miracle question (Sharry, et al. 2001) it is used to:

- Bypass problem thinking.
- Create a context for setting (well formed) goals.
- Encourage expectations of change.
- Get information about how progress can be made.
- Find out about behaviours that will complete the work.

I allowed a full 25 minutes for this exercise. Question 4 in the Time Quake script enabled them to have a definite bench mark on progress and to appreciate how they had got there. Clearly, the next logical question (to be asked later in the plenary) was, 'What would you have to do to get half a point higher up the scale?'

The result of Time Quake was to give real hope and grounds for optimism. I noticed, especially, that the two participants whom I discerned at the start to be mildly clinically depressed, looked somewhat bright. In the plenary, gathering information on the two groups' five questions in turn, a mass of detail emerged.

At this point, the four flip chart sheets I had taped together end to end, with a time line and pinned to the wall earlier, came into their own:

TIME LINE CHART

1999	2000	Now ↑ (2002)	2003

Figure 5 – Time line chart

It proved to be very helpful to all concerned to mark up what had been achieved up until the time of the workshop.

Small steps

The two groups were moved immediately into another 25-minute exercise. In addition to asking what had been achieved so far, I asked them to think also what other small steps might well be achieved over the next three months or so.

A chart of trigger questions for this exercise was provided as follows (Figure 6):

a) What is working well at present?
b) What gives us most hope?
c) What is 'in the bag' so far?
d) What do we know will be 'in the bag'?
e) What small steps will we take over (say) the next 3 months or so?
f) How have we helped to support and re-motivate each other to date?

Figure 6 – Trigger Questions

On the time line chart in Figure 5, we were able to plot what had happened and when and who was responsible for each achievement. In plotting these events, I made the mistake of using ancient milestones of the following design (Figure 7):

Figure 7 – Milestone or tombstone?

The morbid thinking and dark humour amongst some participants prompted the comment: 'He's drawn tombstones!' Naturally, they were changed immediately to straight, modern looking posts!

Having marked the past, present, and a little piece of the future, I moved them into a further future focus by the following brainstorming exercise:

Milestones – the next 12 months

We began quickly to fill in the months well into the future, as a lot of energy was created by this exercise. In good SF tradition, concerning the characteristics of small steps, I ensured that each marker on the time line chart was annotated with lots of detail – who, what, when, how? This would be useful later.

Going forward from here

By this point, which by now was near the workshop's end, participants had become energised; they had been encouraged by their own declared strengths and resources; they became more hopeful about the future; and most importantly, had a clearer idea about the small steps each needed to take. Indeed, these were now all clearly marked on the time line.

It was emphasised that this workshop had not been a 'shallow, make-happy' exercise. Instead, it was both a more serious appreciation of their concerns in the present situation and their realistic hopes for a better future. It had served as a purposeful, helpful and constructive look at what can and will be achieved in the months ahead, once they pull more together as a team.

As the workshop ended, there was a noticeable buzz, endorsed by a noticeably stronger and more positive body language.

Outcome

The HoDs team were remotivated greatly by the workshop and, according to the GM, went on to develop many small income-generating projects during the shutdown period. A fortnight later, a similar result was achieved for the rest of the workforce remnant of some 14 employees. As a larger group, HoDs and workers together were able to maintain their own and each other's morale during a very lean period in the company's history. Not only did they survive the shutdown, but went on to win other projects for the longer term. The financial backer of the main project released the money after 11 months and the workforce is now almost back up to full strength.

Conclusion

This case is a good example of how to use the SF process model to achieve a desired outcome in a very time limited way. Whilst it is important to hear out the problem sufficiently, acknowledging and validating all feelings expressed, we find it unhelpful to dwell on problem talk for too long before moving people on.

SF facilitations of this sort are neither about starting from scratch, nor about producing a complete solution to a problem situation. It is more about firstly flagging up what has already been (and is being) achieved, before identifying what keys need to be put in place to complete the solution building process. Secondly, once tasks and appropriate timescales have been identified, it is then the facilitator's job to empower the team further, to put it all into practice.

References

Jackson, Paul Z and McKergow, Mark (2002), *The Solutions Focus: The Simple Way to Positive Change*, Nicholas Brealey Publishing

Cameron, Esther (1998), *Facilitation Made Easy*, London, Kogan Page.

Dolan, Yvonne (2000), *Beyond Survival: Living Well is the Best Revenge*, London, BT Press.

Miller, Scott D, Hubble, M and Duncan, B (1996), *Handbook of Solution Focused Brief Therapy*, San Francisco, Jossey-Bass.

Sharry, John, Madden, B and Darmody, M (2001), *Becoming a Solutions Detective: A Strengths Based Guide to Brief Therapy*, London, BT Press.

Biographical note

John Henden is Managing Director of John Henden Consultancy Ltd, a solution focused consultancy, and is a trainer, facilitator and management coach. For over 20 years, he worked within NHS mental health services. He provides consultancy, training and facilitation across a wide range of organisations and industries. John has a background in psychology and is a presenter at, and member of, the European Brief Therapy Association. He is also on the steering group of SOL (Solutions in Organisations Link-up), the international SF practitioners' network.

Tel: +44 (0) 1823 333183
e-mail: john@johnhendenconsultancy.co.uk
www.johnhendenconsultancy.co.uk

Originally published in Organisations and People, Volume 16, Number 4, pages 12–18.

About Solutions Focused Scaling:

10 minutes for Performance and Learning

Peter Szabó

The best opportunities for personal performance improvement usually happen during daily work situations, if these opportunities are used for learning. Solutions Focused scaling questions help to make the most of these learning opportunities in less than ten minutes. The questions are simple to ask, easy to slip into any professional conversation and they have been proven to work. You can use them on yourself or to facilitate performance and learning for others.

The basics of scaling

Scaling is probably the easiest tool in the Solutions Focused model for immediate application. The most commonly used scales within Solutions Focused conversations are the progress scale (see example below) and the confidence scale (on a scale from 0 to 10, how confident are you that you will accomplish the next small step towards your goal?). Of course many other kinds of scales can be invented and utilised: customer service quality scales, motivation scales, core competency scales etc. (see Berg and Steiner 2003:107 for creative scaling applications).

Example: Progress Scale

'Let's take a scale from 0 to 10. 10 stands for having completely reached your goal and 0 stands for the moment when you first started to think about this goal. Where would you say things are between 0 and 10 right now?'

Scaling questions can serve four major purposes:

1. **Giving hope and confidence in what has already been accomplished**

   Usually answers are above 0 allowing you to focus on the things that already work – even a little bit. Asking *'How is your answer different from 0?'* is an invitation for solution-talk. Whatever is said in response helps to build confidence and hope about things that have already improved. It helps to focus on the distance already travelled and to better understand the useful activities that made it possible: *'How did you do that?'*

2. **Offering shades of gray**

   Scaling can help to introduce observable differences between what seems either black or white. Often it is useful to ask: *'How is your point on the scale different today from yesterday or how is it different in this project compared to that one?'* The invitation is designed to find relevant differences that really make a difference. Once detected these differences can consciously be used to extend and build on existing solutions.

3. **Focusing on small next steps**

   Whatever the actual position on the scale, a very important move is the next small step upwards. Asking *'How will you notice that you have moved up one point on your scale?'* is an invitation to focus the attention on observable signs of progress and improvement. Followed by *'and what else?'*, it opens up a range of options and ideas for small and realistic things to do differently.

4. **Considering consequences of having reached the goal**

   Scales help to define the wanted state. Some people want to reach 10, while for others reaching 7 or 8 is exactly where they want to be. Asking *'How will things be different when you have reached your goal on the scale?'* uncovers what people will be doing differently then that they are not doing now. The more the described future activities are concretely embedded into the real life situation, the more they can function as signposts for improved performance.

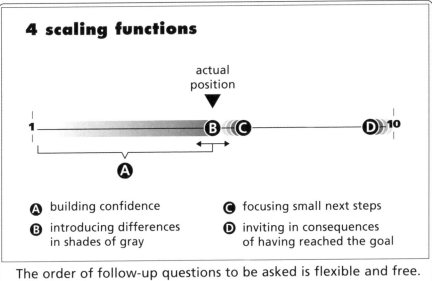

4 scaling functions

actual position

1 — Ⓑ Ⓒ — Ⓓ 10

Ⓐ

Ⓐ building confidence   Ⓒ focusing small next steps
Ⓑ introducing differences   Ⓓ inviting in consequences
   in shades of gray   of having reached the goal

The order of follow-up questions to be asked is flexible and free. Scales are a perfect means to surf ahead on solutions like a surfer would do with his surfboard on a wave in the ocean.

Figure 1

Seven principles for Solutions Focused scaling

1. **Be respectful**
    Remember to ask for permission if you have no mandate to work on performance and learning. If there is no request for help, do not help. If something works do not fix it. Ask your partner: 'What would be helpful to you?'

2. **Set a clear learning frame**
    Create a distinct difference between 'solution-surfing' and the normal 'getting the job done' talk with content discussions, tips and to do lists. Sometimes the mere using of scales creates this difference. Sometimes putting a scalingboard (like the Rickter Scale (www.rickterscale.com) or the Skaleboard (www.solutionsurfers.com)) on the table, or drawing a scale on the flip-chart is a clear enough visual signal. Do whatever it takes to support your partner shifting from action mode to reflection mode.

3. **Go with what is said**
    Solutions in learning and individual assessments of it are surprisingly subjective. They are most effective when left at that very personal insight level. Bringing in your own view into someone else's reflection mode leads to endless and useless discussions. Remind yourself that you are not asking questions to receive an answer but to provide learning and reflection time for your partner.

4. **Appreciate what is there**
    Phrase your scaling questions in a way to generate information about existing resources and exceptions that already work. Remember that solution talk creates solutions, while talking about deficits and problems makes problems bigger.

5. **Look for differences**
    Absolute figures like scales (or grades) are – as you may remember from school – not so relevant for learning. What really makes a difference is being aware of differences between figures, giving relevant information about what really works.

6. **Count to 20**

   Scaling questions can be unusual and difficult since they introduce a new and different way of thinking. So give your partner enough time for learning reflection. Count to 20 while you are waiting for an answer and when you reach 20, count again.

7. **Stop after 10 minutes**

   No matter how tempting it may be to go on, 10 minutes usually provide more than enough reflection material to be put into action steps. Remember that reflecting on performance is just as strenuous as it is fulfilling.

Performance improvement through learning on the job

Challenges that you are currently facing in your job provide optimal opportunities for improving your own performance – like in a huge 24-hour multimedia sensurround seminar that was just set up for your learning, with unlimited funds for stage setting, brilliant scripts and talented actors. The sequencing of the plot is tailored for the benefit of your best possible improvement. All experiences are directly transferable to make your next project even more successful. Management Coach Timothy Gallwey (Gallwey 2000:88) simply asks: 'In this seminar called "your life" are you enrolled as a learner?'

There are three major factors to consider when looking for positive change in your real life/work situation:

- the clarity of your vision about what you want to achieve ('future perfect', Jackson and McKergow, 2002) at the right end of the scale
- the extent to which first steps are concretely designed ('small next step')

- and finally the extent of belief that it can be done (valuing all the 'counters' that are present in the left range of the scale)

This is why scaling proves to be so effective. In less than ten minutes, scaling questions can generate useful perceptions and relevant information necessary to start improvement.

Scaling questions to get you started

1. On a scale from 0 to 10, to what extent do you take advantage of learning opportunities in your job?
   - What accounts for the difference between your answer and 0?
   - And what do you do to support this learning?
2. On the same scale, where would you like things to be?
   - What would you do differently as a consequence of having reached that level?
3. Suppose time goes by and you move one step higher on the same scale, what would tell you that you had accomplished that one small step?

Using scaling with teams

Jane is the new leader of a quality management team. She wants to improve the effectiveness of the team meetings she leads and is using scales for on the job learning.

Asking for direct feed forward

Before closing the regular weekly team meeting Jane allows ten minutes of Solutions Focused process reflection:

'On a scale from 0 to 10 how effective have we been as a team in reaching our goals for the meeting?'

Being used to this type of questions Bill answers:

'To me it was a 5. And what made it a 5 was that I appreciated how we clearly and quickly postponed discussion of the 3rd topic since nobody was really prepared.'

The other team members also give their ratings and thoughts. And Jane marks everybody's answer on a large scale drawn on the flip chart. She also writes down helpful contributions.

In less than ten minutes, Jane accomplished at least three things:

- She made everybody conscious that effectiveness is a learning issue for the team.
- She positively reinforced people and actions that contributed to the effectiveness of the meeting, providing learning about what works.
- She learned about the things that were considered helpful by her team members.

When applying scaling questions with teams it is important not to get stuck in debating figures or looking for agreement about the ratings. The absolute ratings are used only to elicit relevant information about whatever was working in the meeting. It is not important whether an individual team member rates the scale at 3 or 9.

Where most of the ratings turn out to be low (e.g. below 3), it makes sense of course to go with the team flow and spend less time with what DID work and more time with what needs to be learned by the team and how it could get just one point higher on the scale.

Preparing next work/learning steps

At the beginning of the next team meeting Jane posts the flip chart again.

> 'This is what we said at the end of the last meeting and now I am curious how effective we will be this time. Knowing our agenda for today and knowing how we work together as a team, please give me your guess of what you will say at the end of this meeting about our team effectiveness? And how will you know?'

Jane marks the guessed figures with a different colour on the flip chart. She also writes down information given by each team member about necessary actions and the stated positive consequences of reaching the respective effectiveness level. For example, from Paula's contribution, she notes: 'First discuss what needs to happen with a topic on the agenda – getting to the point faster.'

These five minutes of introduction may prove helpful to

- focus the team members' attention on a learning goal
- create a range of options for useful actions to be taken during the meeting
- elicit a motivating image of how well the meeting could go.

Focusing on what worked

At the end of the meeting Jane takes another five minutes for performance assessment:

> 'Looking at where we were during the last meeting and how we did today: what has become better on our team effectiveness scale? Where would you say we are now?'

Paula's overall rating at 8 is even higher than her guess of 7. Several times she herself had helped the team to clarify the goal. On the other hand Bill scores at 4, lower than last time. He is disappointed about the length of individual statements and overall discussions.

Jane understands his frustration and asks him:

> 'Any ideas on how we managed not to fall below 4? What did we do today that worked even a little bit to keep statements and discussions no lower than 4?'

Jane might choose to bring up the effectiveness scale again sometime later. Since the team is familiar with this way of working, her next scaling inquiry could be as short as half a minute.

Celebrating moments of excellence

In the middle of a next team meeting all of a sudden Jane senses that the team is buzzing. She asks the team to hold it just for a short moment of effectiveness rating:

> 'Let's just take a quick round with team effectiveness ratings for these last 5 minutes, how are we doing on a scale from 0 to 10, everybody?'

Usually there is no need to spend time on what the individual ratings mean. A quick round with just a figure stated is all it takes to shift into learning mode and enjoyment.

Of course this inquiry can also be used when things do not seem to be going so well. Jane might use it in a not-knowing way to find out whether she is the only one subjectively suffering an apparent lack of effectiveness. She might also use the question deliberately to remind the team that this unpleasant experience could be used for learning. Again a short shift of awareness is usually more than sufficient to provide learning and potential change – so it is OK to just get back to regular work discussion after the round and maybe do another round later when helpful differences become noticable.

Using scaling with individuals

Jane's boss, Alan, is a natural in scaling using scales in his conversations with simplicity and ease.

So here are some of Alan's favourite applications with individuals.

a) defining the learning goal

In one of the first meetings with Jane, Alan wants to know which learning opportunities are important to her in her new job. She lists several things that she is eager to learn more about. One of these is how to lead effective team meetings because she had suffered with lousy meetings led by her former boss. To help Jane define her learning goals, Alan asks the following two scaling questions:

'Take a scale from 0 to 10 with 10 standing for the most effective team meetings that could ever be led and 0 standing for the opposite. How high do you want to get with your learning on this scale?'

While Jane's answer is an 8, the figure for the goal may vary from person to person and from learning topic to learning topic. So it makes sense to go with whatever figure is stated.

'What will you be doing at 8 that you are not doing now in your team meetings?'

It is important at this stage to relate the learning goal to realistic actions in the learner's real environment. It was at this point that Jane successfully started to develop some ideas to put into action at the next team meeting. All Alan had to do was to ask an occasional: 'What else?' in order to increase her options for improvement. In Jane's case, Alan had every reason to trust that her ideas were realistic even for the next team meeting. If there had been any doubt he could have wrapped up at the end with:

'You have clearly defined many things that you would do at 8. So tell me what level on the scale seems realistic to you for the next meeting and which things would you do at that level?'

Note that even though Alan is Jane's boss, he lets her define how far SHE wants to get with her learning and which next steps SHE wants to take. So using scales to facilitate learning can be a somewhat different conversation from regular managerial discussions. As manager he typically talks about what needs to be done in order to get results (What do we need to do to get there?). When using his learning scales, he often asks about the consequences of having reached the result (What will you be doing differently after you have reached your goal?). He wants to make progress credible and thus possible before it becomes clear how to get there.

b) Introducing differences

Next time she sees Alan, Jane brings up her experiences with the last team meeting. Her overall rating of how she did as leader of the meeting is at 6. Alan congratulates her and asks:

'I'd love to know some details, so tell me about two specific moments during the meeting, one where you were clearly above 6 and one where you were not so happy with your performance'

Jane takes some time to think and then comes up with a conflict situation at 3 and a moment that was at ten. Of course Alan is Solutions Focused enough to be curious what made the 10 to be a 10. To discover more information about the differences that made a difference to Jane he asks her:

'What exactly did you do at 10 that you did not do at 3?'

The more specific a description of concrete activities, the more options for future steps become available to the learner. And since there is such a huge gap between 3 and 10, Alan could also chunk down and ask Jane how the situation with the 3 would be different after just taking a small step towards 4.

c) *Changing perspective*

One way of defining learning is putting more appropriate ideas into ACTION. So in most cases for learning to happen there should be a clearly visible difference observable from the outside. Therefore it is useful to introduce the perception of an outside observer into the scaling questions from time to time. For teams this perspective can be the focus of internal or external customers. In Jane's case it could be her team, or Alan her boss, or her custumers in one of her projects.

So continuing the conversation Alan asks Jane:

'What will be the first small sign your most sensitive team member would notice during the next conflict situation that would tell him or her that you have moved from 3 to 4?'

d) *Focusing on the distance travelled*

The next encounter beween Jane and her boss is a short one. They walk past each other in the middle of a long hallway and both just have one minute to spare. Jane says that she is on her way to a project meeting that she will be leading. With a broad smile on his face Alan points to the two ends of the hallway and says:

'OK Jane, this is a walking scale. That end of the hallway that you came from is 0 meaning the moment when you first started to think about learning how to lead meetings effectively and that end over there that you are heading towards stands for 10. Where are you right now on your personal progress scale?'

Jane smiles as she walks way past Alan. Continuing almost all the way down the hallway she finally stops and shouts: 'This is where I am, Alan!' He quickly checks her total distance travelled and esti-mates an 8. 'Time to move on to new learnings Jane, don't you think!' he replies.

Nine and a half

To move half a point higher on the scale in your own learning, you might want to try some of the ideas here. Most people who have experienced scaling questions find they give more visual and emotional clarity, a sense of precision and a high concentration of thought. Most new practitioners of Solutions Focused conversations will appreciate scaling questions since they make it easier to get to the point and to stay with the client's perception.

However, you don't have to believe this! Please find out for yourself and learn more about what is useful about scaling for you. Make sure to regularly ask your conversation partners:

'By the way, how useful is this conversation for you on a scale from 0 to 10? What is useful and how can we make it even more useful for you?'

References
Berg, Insoo Kim and Steiner, Therese (2003), *Children's Solution Work*, New York, Norton & Company.

Gallwey, Timothy W (2000), *The Inner Game of Work*, New York, Random House.

Jackson, Paul Z and McKergow Mark (2002), *The Solutions Focus*, London, Nicholas Brealey Publishing.

Biographical note

Peter Szabó trains SF coaches at the Weiterbildungsforum in Basel, Switzerland (www.weiterbildungsforum.ch). Currently he is involved in creating the SolutionSurfers Foundation which plans to support and further SF research, training and tools within the business world (www.solutionsurfers.com).

Unt. Batterieweg 73, 4059 Basel, Tel/Fax +41 61 361 11 88
Email: szabo@bluewin.ch

Originally published in Organisations and People, Volume 10, Number 4, pages 19–26.

Solution Focused Reflecting Teams in Action

Harry Norman with Michael Hjerth and Tim Pidsley

Much of the background to Solutions Focus comes from use with individuals. This article presents a format for using the resources and knowledge present within a team. Solution Focused Reflecting Teams is in use internationally and in many contexts, as Harry Norman and his colleagues show.

Solution Focused Reflecting Teams (SFR Teams) offer groups and teams a way of conducting useful meetings where time is at a premium and the team has the confidence and the wish to utilise the experience, resources and skills within the team. This way of working developed during the meetings of Bristol Solutions Group (BSG), a group interested in Solution Focused thinking and practice and self-managed learning. BSG experimented with Reflecting Team ideas (Andersen 1991) and a time-limited Solution Focused reflective way of working started to emerge. Harry Norman, one of the founders of BSG, was curious about this and discussed it with the rest of the group. The group continued to experiment and, after a while, brought news of SFR Teams to a conference in a workshop. The workshop resonated with the Solution Focused community and soon people started approaching Harry at conferences, telling him about the ways they were using SFR Teams. Now, traditional ongoing teams, cross-functional teams and project teams are using SFR Teams. Trainers use SFR Teams as a training tool. SFR Teams are used by teams for problem solving, by expert consulting teams, by learning sets, peer mentoring groups, and also business support groups. Doubtless there are other applications already 'out there'!

SFR Teams operate in a resource focused way even if the team members have no pre-existing Solution Focused skills. The SFR Team format is an analogue of a solution-focused coaching process – a cycle of *preparing, presenting, clarifying, affirming, reflecting and closing*. The client or 'customer for receiving help' makes some kind of *preparation* for the coaching session. This may vary from having some idea about what the meeting could be about to writing a report on progress made since a previous meeting. The customer tells their story (*presents*) and explains what he or she wants some help with. The coach asks questions to *clarify* what is hoped for, who is involved, progress already made, and the skills, abilities and resources the customer brings to the situation. The coach *affirms* the customer's relevant skills, abilities and resources, by offering relevant and pertinent compliments. The coach considers 'the story so far' and *reflects* on ways that the customer could make further progress. The coach and the customer *close* the meeting by discussing how the customer could make progress after the session.

Solution focused reflecting team structure

Phase	Activities	Listening & speaking rules
PREPARING	Each person who hopes to receive help prepares for the meeting and is clear about what they hope to gain from the meeting.	
PRESENTING	Team members take it in turns to receive help. The customer for receiving help describes the situation they would like some help with.	Only the customer speaks. When there is written preparation the customer may elect to have another team member read the preparation out loud.
CLARIFYING	The team is interested in clarifying the story so far and interested in the customer's skills, abilities, resources and achievements. Questions for clarification are encouraged – e.g. 'What?', 'When?', 'Where?, 'Who?' and 'How?' based questions. 'Why?' questions and closed questions are discouraged. It is not necessary for team members to ask questions that build a theme or thread.	Team members each take a turn to ask one question and one follow-up question, and then remain silent until their turn comes around again.

Phase	Activities	Listening & speaking rules
AFFIRMING	The team members tell the customer briefly what impresses each of them most about him, or her, in the situation they have described. Team members may offer similar compliments.	The team members speak in any order. The customer remains silent.
REFLECTING	Each team member says one thing at a time or 'passes'. Sometimes team members offer reflections triggered by previous reflections. The team continues until everyone has said all they want to say, or time runs out.	The team members speak in sequence. The customer remains silent. (If the team's reflections are clearly and persistently based on a misunderstanding the customer may speak very briefly to point this out.)
CLOSING	The customer responds briefly to what was said in the reflecting phase, usually stating what seems most applicable and specifies some course of action.	Only the customer speaks.

Clarifying

Questions for clarifying are encouraged during the clarification phase – questions that begin 'What?' 'When?' 'Where?' 'Who?' and 'How?' as they provide descriptions of what has already taken place. 'Why' based questions and closed questions are discouraged as they tend to stimulate theory driven inquiry rather than curiosity driven questioning (O'Hanlon and Wilk, 1987). Teams sometimes ponder whether a particular question is 'truly a clarification question'. For instance, 'What are you most optimistic about?' can be regarded as going beyond clarification because it shifts the focus to the future and solution building – different teams reach different conclusions about this. Questions that begin 'I wonder' are best kept as material for the reflecting phase.

Reflecting

Each team member offers only one reflection at a time. (Each reflection sounds more like a sentence than a paragraph!) As 'bad news' hinders the flow of reflections it is best to offer any legalistic issues, negative feedback or concerns at the beginning of the reflecting phase, then the team can establish a 'flow'. The team's rate of speech often slows down during this phase and pauses between reflections are common. (Often, when this happens the team members are leaning back in their chairs.) Reflections of team members often build on the previous reflections of other team members. Team members sometimes pose 'rhetorical questions' in the form of 'I wonder if you might xyz?' for the customer to ponder. The customer remains silent throughout the reflecting phase.

SFR Teams are usually between five and eight members. Each customer taking a 'turn' receives help for a maximum of half an hour. Thus a team session for five members, each taking a turn, needs two and a half hours. When planning a half-hour turn, time the phases something like this; Presenting – four minutes, Clarifying – ten minutes, Affirming – two minutes, Reflecting – ten minutes, Closing – four minutes. Michael Hjerth, from Stockholm, tells us that when in doubt he shortens the presenting phase to one sentence; this improves the quality of the clarification phase and leaves customers just as satisfied. It is common for some customers to feel that they need more time to present, and also some team members wish for more time to offer more input. However, sticking to a maximum of half an hour works very well – especially if the team persists and gains experience of working this way. Rationing each team member's input can accommodate larger teams (e.g. one question and one reflection per team member).

SFR teams and learning sets

Self-Managed Learning (SML) is increasingly used in training and development. It has the benefit of closely integrating personal and organisational goals, practical application and reflection, individual and shared responsibility (Cunningham, 1999). A key element in successful SML is the effective functioning of the 'Learning Set' or 'Learning Group'. Effective Learning Sets create a true 'learning environment' in which individuals can reflect on their learning, and develop their practice. Responsibility for action remains with the individual but they are able to rehearse and reflect within the learning set in addition to getting practical input and sharing ideas. The needs and priorities of individuals are usually detailed in a 'Learning Contract'. Part of the role of the learning set is to support and challenge individuals in the implementation of their contract. This focus on the specific helps to ensure that sustainable change takes place. Typically set meetings are divided into individual timeslots. Prior to the meeting, members decide how they wish to make use of their timeslot. They may choose to present some information, lead a discussion, ask for ideas and input, share difficulties and challenges, or anything else, provided it is directed towards helping them to fulfil their learning contract. During these timeslots the full attention of set members is focused on the particular circumstances and needs of one of their number. After the meeting set members then reflect on the input and insights from the meeting and how they can use them to assist in implementing their learning contract.

Tim Pidsley, from Llandeillo, uses SFR Teams as a communication framework with Learning Sets. He points out some parallels between SFR Teams and typical learning sets:

- The discrete periods of time focussing on one individual.
- The requirement to do some preparation beforehand.
- The sense of leaving responsibility for action with the individual.

Individuals involved in learning sets using SFR Teams have also identified advantages. 'It means that the format of the discussion is known in advance and everyone will have an equal opportunity to contribute both their own "problem" and their thoughts on other people's.' And 'It gives a structure to the thinking and a springboard to ideas.'

Usually learning sets meet every four to eight weeks over a period of months. Initially participants feel constrained by the discipline of the SFR Team format. However, they adapt to the structure, and find that the boundaries and time constraints actually work to their advantage. Adopting the SFR Team communication framework helps ensure that there is equality of contribution and attention for each set member. At a practical level the available time for the set meeting can be divided into equal chunks. SFR Teams require that the team focuses on one person's issues at a time – this prevents the process being hi-jacked. Additionally, everyone knows that there will be a time when the set's focus is on their issue and so they are more prepared to suspend their own needs in order to help their fellow set member. The limited time for each of the phases encourages focus amongst the whole of the set. The customer has to decide what they do and don't want to share, and often doesn't have time to give much background. The limited time for clarifying encourages the team members to ask their most important questions first, as they might not get another turn! The briefness of the affirming phase encourages the delivery of the most valuable compliments. The dynamics of the 'reflecting' phase are slightly different as the opportunity to 'pass', and the reasonable likelihood of being able to make a number of contributions, enables building on 'reflections' that others have offered.

The expectation of a response from the customer in the 'closing' phase means the customer has to speak fairly spontaneously. This may seem unfair, but in practice an immediate response often means the customer picks out the most useful and significant ideas. The time-limited aspect of SFR Teams is one which sets find initially most constraining. As a set adviser it has been interesting for Tim to observe how sets grow into the use of SFR Teams. Initially, they genuinely seem to have too little time for each phase but, with practice, as their focus and communication skills develop, he has noticed sets running out of questions to ask or things to say before the time for each phase is complete! When questioning individuals about this, Tim has often had the response 'Well, I did have more to say, but I'd said what I thought were the most significant things and wanted to leave it at that.'

SFR teams and business support

Harry Norman has used SFR Teams with businesses and business start-ups. This has included ongoing learning sets as well as one-off groups convened at conferences. A typical ongoing business or enterprise support group (ESG) consists of five people with differ-ent kinds of roles or businesses. Reported benefits of ESGs include; efficient use of time, structured and focused meetings, useful busi-ness development ideas, progress with specific issues, better focus, improved meetings skills, increased confidence and self-belief, increased revenue, and also the companionship and understanding of peers. Typically, an ESG meets every four to eight weeks and each member brings written preparation (one side of a piece of paper maximum). The ESG members take turns to receive support and each presentation phase consists only of reading out the written preparation. The group reviews progress every six months – prepa-ration for this meeting consists of reviewing the last six months and looking forward six months. At this meeting the group decides whether to continue for another six months.

SFR teams as a training tool

As the SFR Teams format is a transparent deconstruction of the Solution Focused interactional cycle, Michael Hjerth uses SFR Teams as a training tool for Solution Focused skills. By using SFR Teams participants learn important aspects of interviewing in general, and Solution Focused interviewing in particular. Training with SFR Teams helps people to focus on just one thing at a time. There are three main benefits from using SFR Teams in training contexts:

- Enhanced knowledge sharing.
- A clear process model for knowledge-building to take home.
- Because of the transparent format, SFR Team sessions can easily be adapted to other contexts.

Some of the skills SFR Teams help develop are

1. **Listening quietly instead of directing the inquiry process.**
   The clarification phase discipline of taking turns to ask questions encourages team members to pay close attention to the flow of answers to questions, and this stimulates team-driven curiosity.
2. **Resisting the urge to offer solutions early in the process.**
   The clarification phase discipline of asking clarifying questions ('What?' 'When?' 'Where?' 'Who?' and 'How?' based questions), inhibit premature theory building and the rush to offer advice.
3. **Positive Feedback Skills.**
   Each team member knows that the clarification phase is followed by offering the customer compliments. This feeding-forward skews the questioning in the direction of confirming, or discovering, skills, abilities and resources which can be built upon. In a peer support session each member of the team practises offering and receiving compliments.

The Falk Team

The Falk Team in Uppsala, Sweden, was formed to help occupational rehabilitation caseworkers find ways forward with clients who have got 'stuck'. The Falk Team is a cross-organisational expert group, whose members consist of one specialist from each of Employment Services, Social Security, Social Services, Primary Health Care and Psychiatric Services. Despite initial reluctance, the Falk Team tried out SFR Teams as a team consultation model. Their reluctance was partly due to typical Swedish diffidence about compliments and partly due to disquiet about possible conflicts. (In situations where caseworkers have got stuck, the responsibilities and interests of the organisations involved often become confused and sometimes they conflict.) However it was agreed that occupational rehab caseworkers from these organisations could book a consultation and become the 'customer' in an SFR Falk Team. A year later they were still using SFR Teams. In interviews about the process, customers said things like 'I was less defensive after the compliments' and 'The compliments helped me consider their ideas more closely'. The obligation to compliment the customer helps ensure that the customer is perceived (by the team) as having done their best, and the customer is made aware of this perception. This makes it easier for the customer to entertain new possible courses of action, even if 'the enemy' has suggested them!

The Falk Team have returned to Tom Andersen's original reflecting team idea that the customer literally takes a step back while the team members reflect among themselves – so the customer eavesdrops on the team's reflections. The customer is told that their job is to sit back and listen for anything that might be useful and ignore anything that might not be useful. The customer decides whether to make any notes. The team facilitator (or peer co-ordinator) keeps an eye on the team to make sure that reflections are directed only to the team. Michael Hjerth reports that this procedure 'super-charges' the reflections. 'The more closely we follow the rule of keeping the reflections in-team, the more interested the customer seems to be.'

The Falk Team is satisfied with the results from using SFR Team consultancy sessions. They say that they understand better how each organisation works and have a better understanding of each other. They say they see more possibilities for collaboration and their work has become more focused on clients and less focused on the organisations involved. The Falk Team customers feel more able to continue to work with cases where previously they were close to giving up. They say this is because they can see new possibilities, or they now see they were doing better than they originally thought they were doing!

How do SFR teams work?

I have developed ideas that often seem simpleminded. I believe in simplicity and in systems theory. And I take both seriously. (*de Shazer 1986*)

When I think about how SFR Teams work I often remember this sentence because when I start to think about 'simplicity' and 'systems theory', things seem to get complicated. Initially it seems obvious that the customer picks out some useful suggestions for future action during the reflecting phase. Clearly this is one way SFR Teams do work – however some customers report that the compliments offered in the affirming phase stimulate them to new actions that weren't even discussed at the meeting.

SFR Teams involve team members in offering and considering positive feedback. These skills seem to be greatly neglected arts. Positive feedback can let us know what others would like from us more often. In a more personal way, the idiosyncratic and personal pleasure we get from engaging in activities or relationships that gladden our hearts is a kind of positive feedback which can help us each decide as individuals to 'Do more of this.'

In an ongoing team, the team members refresh their relationships through the practice of offering and receiving compliments, and in teams that don't come together every day the disciplined structure and compliments involved in SFR Teams help create a team focus, and feeling, very quickly.

References

Andersen, T (1991) *The Reflecting Team: Dialogues and Dialogues About the Dialogues*, New York, WW Norton.

Cunningham, I (1999), *The Wisdom of Strategic Learning*, London, Gower Publishing Limited.

de Shazer, S 1986, *Utilization: The Foundation of Solutions*, pp. 112–124, 'Developing Ericksonian Therapy', New York, Brunnel Mazel.

O'Hanlon, WH, and Wilk, J (1987), *Shifting Contexts: The Generation of Effective Psychotherapy*, New York, Guilford Press.

Biographical note

Harry Norman, co-founder of the Bristol Solutions Group, has been involved in Solution Focused thinking and practice since 1991. He devised and ran the world's first Solutions Coaching course in 1996 and also developed the Solution Focused Reflecting Team model. Harry works with individuals, teams and organisations for fun, learning and money. Visit www.solutionsology.co.uk or email him at support@solutionsology.co.uk.

Michael Hjerth is part of the team of trainers, educators and supervisors at FKC and Solutionwork (www.solutionwork.com) in Sweden. He specialises in management and leadership, organisational development and team building, is Secretary to the European Brief Therapy Association and has a background in philosophy and language. Email him at michael.hjerth@fkc.se.

Tim Pidsley works as an independent people and organisation development consultant. Among his interests are team and workgroup development and the individual and organisational benefits that can be derived from their effective functioning. He enjoys helping people find and implement solutions to their workplace issues thereby improving things for themselves, for those they serve and for their organisation. His work in the private sector is done primarily through Minerva Consulting (www.minervaconsulting.co.uk), and in the health sector through The Centre for Health Leadership Wales (www.chl.wales.nhs.uk). He can be contacted directly on Tim.Pidsley@orange.net.

Originally published in Organisations and People, Volume 10, Number 4, pages 27–33.

Solution Focused Rating (SFR):

New Ways in Performance Appraisal

Dr. Günter Lueger

Performance appraisal is one area where a problem focus is often taken, unwittingly, in an attempt to improve performance. Here Günter Lueger considers how to bring a solutions focus to performance management, and presents a novel yet simple approach for building solutions talk within an appraisal interview.

Introduction

Performance appraisal is the ongoing process of evaluating and managing both behaviour and outcome in the workplace (Carrell et al. 1995:348). Many decisions like staffing, defining training needs, direction for future performance, feedback, etc., are based on the evaluation of job performance. It is one of the most important fields of human resource management and leadership and is used in almost all companies with professional human resource systems.

It is somewhat surprising that this critical field is still a muddy area of personnel management. Findings show that a lot of companies report dissatisfaction with their performance appraisal systems (Bernardin et al. 1995).

This article will show that many existing problems are caused by a problem-centred view in appraisal systems and appraisal interviews. One of the most critical problems can be found in the rating instrument and the classic rating scales. It will be demonstrated that classic rating instruments make change of behaviour and performance more difficult and lead to conflicts in interviews.

This article presents a new solution-oriented rating instrument (SFR) and alternative attitudes for raters which allow a Solution Focused process in performance appraisal and appraisal interviews.

Reasons for dissatisfaction with performance appraisal

The evaluation of performance appraisal systems is not very widespread in human resource management but it is important for the effectiveness of such systems (Coens and Jenkins 2002). Managers in companies very often assume that performance appraisal is a good way of achieving objectives and leads to change of behaviour and acceptance of ratings by the ratee.

But surveys conducted to shed light on the satisfaction of raters, ratees and administrators of performance appraisal systems show different results (Bernardin et al. 1995:464):

- The majority of people who are rated less than the highest value on a rating scale disagree with the rating more than they agree.
- The majority of the people who disagree with the rating are less motivated and less satisfied with their jobs after the appraisal.
- The majority of these people have little or no idea how to improve their performance.

Thus, the goals of performance appraisal are not achieved especially in those cases in which there is a need for change concerning behaviour or work output. Employees who do not agree with their ratings show little or no willingness to change their behaviour (Murphy 1996).

Very good ratings are well accepted by the employees, but in those cases change is not a priority, anyway.

This lack of acceptance is caused by the way in which the appraisal interviews are carried out as well as by the rating instruments themselves. The interviews tend to focus too much on deficits, weaknesses, and unattained goals – all problems of the past. Instead, as shown below, the interview should concentrate on the employee's resources and questions concerning how to shape the future. Traditional rating instruments are problematic, leading to resistance of change, mainly because they are unlikely take into account the employee's actual performance. This aspect is covered below.

Traditional rating instruments lead to the assumption of stability

The most widely used rating instrument is rating scales (see Figure 1). When raters evaluate performance based on rating scales, they are bound by the instrument to decide on one specific value on the rating scale for the period under review. If, for example, the criterion of 'customer orientation' is rated, the rater has to choose one answer from the scale's alternatives (e.g., 'good', which is then checked). This represents a decision: the employee's customer orientation is 'good', i.e., not 'very good' nor 'average'.

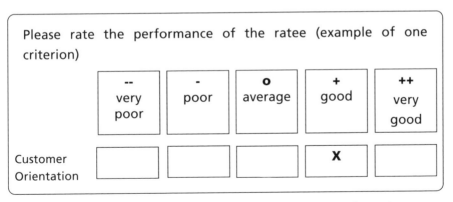

Figure 1 – Traditional rating of a criterion such as customer orientation

The requirement for a specific answer creates a specific 'construction of reality' for the rater, as it induces the rater to assume that the employee's performance is actually the way stated ('good'). As a result, the rater accepts as a fact that the performance under review is CONSTANT over time (see solid line in Figure 2).

Customer Orientation

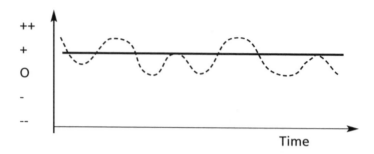

Figure 2 – Performance seen as constant (line) or as varying (curve) through time

It is exactly this issue which lies at the root of acceptance problems an employee may have: an employee's performance and behaviour are NEVER constant over time but vary constantly (there is always change!). At some times, for example, the employee's customer orientation is worse than 'good', while at others it is better, maybe even 'very good' (the curve in Figure 2). Thus, the problem is that the rating instrument does not enable the rater (or the ratee himself or herself in case of self-rating) to reflect actual performance over time.

These problems result in two significant consequences:

1. Conflicts become more probable: if employees are rated 'good', they will tend to quote examples of past performance in their appraisal interview that were better than 'good'; this will – with a high probability – lead the superior to use examples which show less than good performance on the part of the employee. This process will result in a conflict which is difficult to handle and, more importantly, in a situation in which the interview will be confined to past issues (what really happened?). Raters and ratees argue about

reality and do not realise that they themselves are falling victim to the rating system, which simply fails to take into account important variations.

2. Change becomes more difficult: the assumption of stability causes little hope for change. If, for example, the employee is rated 'good', but should show 'very good' behaviour, the following inherent messages are sent to the employee and negatively affect his or her behaviour:

   • The employee has a 'problem', he or she ought to be 'very good' (language creates reality).

   • The employee, not the context, needs to change. This is exactly the opposite of an important principle of the Solution Focused approach which says that 'you have to change something, not someone'. This problem is exacerbated by the fact that many rating instruments feature traits (flexibility, attendance, etc.) as criteria, which focuses the observation in the appraisal even more strongly on the employee at the expense of the context – other factors within the organisation which influence the employee's behaviour (e.g. advertising, ambiguous guidelines for dealing with customers, etc.).

   • The employee needs to do something he or she has not done before (doing something new is always difficult with a view to possible changes).

The problem of 'the best' in traditional rating instruments

All scales contain distinct values, with a best value ('excellent', 'outstanding', etc.) describing the positive end of the scale. There is an inherent assumption that this best value is to be achieved. However, this assumption often proves to be illusory and elusive in many cases. Customer orientation, for example, will be possible only to a limited extent with difficult customers. Similarly, the criterion of 'knowledge' will not always have to be 100% in 100% of cases – while in certain areas extensive knowledge is certainly important, in other areas less detailed knowledge will probably be sufficient. The usually implicit assumption of the need to achieve the best rating value in all fields of work is thus a 'Guide to Unhappiness'. It does not reflect the real work conditions, as there are always situational constraints that make it impossible to fully and completely achieve the best value.

Since this is hardly ever discussed, however, these rating instruments create a 'deficit trance'. A large probability of failure is generated by the appraisal itself (superiors often perceive this difficulty intuitively and rate their employees at the top end of the scale although they know this to be not completely true). Appraisal interviews thus often result in demotivation due to the fact that the rating does not show the best value theoretically possible, although the best value may not be necessary or even be achievable.

Solution Focused rating (SFR): considering differences that make a difference

One very practice-oriented and easily implementable solution to the problems discussed above is a rating which takes into account variations in performance over the period reviewed. Traditional rating instruments can be modified by asking the rater to distribute 100 points across the scale. Figure 3 shows an example of rating, with 10, 70, and 30 points being assigned to 'average', 'good', and 'very good', respectively.

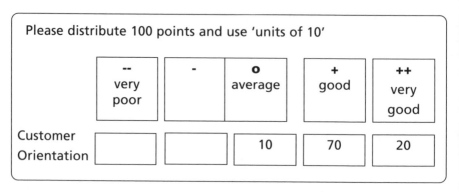

Figure 3 – Example criteria Solution Focused Rating

This modification can easily be applied to existing rating procedures. There is no need for a change of the rating scales, and the
rater only needs to be trained in distributing the points.

The most immediate advantage is the higher probability that the
ratee will accept the rating. The ratee is able to see that the rater
takes into account differences in performance, and in most cases,
includes the top end of the scale in the appraisal.

Above all, however, this makes working out modifications and
improvements considerably easier, as we now have information
which is of greater relevance than is the case with classic instruments. A rating based on SFR makes it easier to focus on what has
to be changed, as it recognises both aspects which need to be
changed and desirable behaviour. We focus on 'the difference that
make a difference' (de Shazer 1997). The appraisal interview can
discuss what works or what does not work. It is evident that the
application of a Solution Focused approach would cause the interview to concentrate on the former (the understanding of the cause of
the problems is not necessary to find solutions – it is a potential
pitfall!). In most instances, the solution is not simply the opposite of
the problem, i.e. what the ratee does to be 'very good' is not the
opposite of 'poor', but something completely different.

A further advantage of SFR is that even small successes on the part of
the ratee are recognised; even if these account for only small percent-
ages at the top or upper end of the scale, they do at least reflect some
success. This signals confidence that change is possible and also
implies that the ratee does have the potential and the resources to
handle tasks even better. The fact that small successes become visible
has one particular effect: the motivation to start a change process.

The appraisal interview will focus on those periods in which the
performance was better than in others. Here, tried and tested questions of the solution-oriented approach (DeJong and Berg 2002) can
be applied. A few examples include the following:

- What would tell you/us that the percentage of 'very good' is
  increasing?

- A score of '70' indicates good consistency. How do you manage that?
- What would be different if the occurrence of 'very good' went up?
- How confident are you about increasing the percentage of 'very good'?

Of course, the variability and the distribution of the values on the scale are not always identical but are subject to significant variations. In most cases, the values on a five-part scale will be distributed among two or three values (as in our example); in rare cases, the distribution may cover all values available. It goes without saying that different criteria will show different distributions for an employee. Thus, the sales generated by a sales assistant may show little variation, while the assistant's co-operation with colleagues may be subject to considerably more variation. Starkly differing results can also be found among employees as regards the distribution of values for the individual criteria.

Small differences are just as valuable as big ones in working out solutions and so focusing on variations provides a wealth of useful information.

Appraisal interview: Solution Focused interviewing

Appraisal interviews represent very challenging and demanding situations for managers and employees and thus require extensive preparation by the rater as well as the ratee. Most appraisal interviews in companies are based on rating instruments, which therefore have a great impact on what can and cannot be discussed in those interviews and thus heavily influence the construction of realities of raters and ratees. Traditional problem-focused questionnaires and rating instruments make it very difficult to avoid using problem talk. Hence – as was shown above – appraisal interviews often result in demotivation on the part of the ratee.

From a solution-oriented perspective, it is clear why difficulties arise in appraisal interviews:

- The share of problem talk is far too high in most interviews: the interview focuses on problems of past performance, on deficits on the employee's part, and on a detailed analysis of the reasons for inadequate performance.
- Many superiors and raters are 'problem screeners' rather than 'solution screeners' and have learned to concentrate on problems (rather than solutions) in the course of interviews.
- The steps for change are described only in vague or fuzzy language.
- The problem is put in terms of what is not wanted.
- The objectives of the interview are not fully clear to the parties, in particular the ratee.

A solution-oriented approach can contribute much to appraisal interviews: doing without a detailed discussion of the employee's deficits and weaknesses, using the areas in which the employee performs well to define clear objectives, and applying the tried and tested interview techniques of the Solution Focused approach.

Traditional approach in appraisal interviews	Solution-oriented approach in appraisal interviews
Brief description, if any, of the interview's objectives.	Extensive discussion of the objectives for rater and ratee.
Standardised interview.	Considering the relationship between rater and ratee (customer, complainant or visitor relationship).
Concentration on the employee's deficits and weaknesses.	Discussion of strengths and small successes and starting points for improvements.
Reduction of the employee's weaknesses by means of personnel development measures.	Making use of strengths by changing work context and job design or staffing.

Traditional approach in appraisal interviews	Solution-oriented approach in appraisal interviews
Tendency to adapt the employee to the work situation.	The work place is also adapted to the employee, and finding solutions is not restricted to unilateral changes but also asks, 'how does it fit?'.
Discussion of problematic details that have occurred in the period under review (usually one year).	Future and goal-orientation.
Definition of vague goals for the upcoming performance period to avoid conflicts.	Above all, objectives are defined specifically and precisely and focus on the presence of things, not their absence.
Superiors and raters make suggestions as to what the ratee should do (which causes the latter to feel unappreciated in his or her capacity to solve problems).	Superior and ratee work out changes together.
Assessment training: focuses on how to use system as intended by the developers of the system.	Assessment training: focuses on solution-orientation and adaptation of the system.
High expectations of appraisal interviews: ideally, all problems will be solved and major progress is made.	Concentration on small and feasible steps that encourage change.
Appreciation – if present at all – is a tool and not an attitude.	Appreciation as an attitude is palpable also in the discussion of common, everyday successes.

Training

Rater training represents an essential success factor for appraisal interviews (as well as rating systems). In the course of rater training, however, raters should be taught not only interview techniques (e.g. exceptions) but also attitudes (goal orientation, amplifying solution talk, ratee as expert, etc.) which help find solutions and useful approaches in the course of appraisal interviews. Training the rater, however, is a part of performance appraisal systems which is often neglected for cost reasons, but this training – as my experience has shown – is one of the most essential elements. Raters tend to rate performance in a manner they have themselves experienced and observed for many years – and this is deficit as well as problem-oriented. Therefore, raters who do not receive training are likely to resort to these language patterns, which, however, can be changed by means of adequate training. If a company is unable to invest large amounts of money in an appraisal system (or its overhaul), it is usually more important to invest in training rather than in the development of appraisal forms and instruments.

Conclusion

Performance appraisal is a field well suited to deploy the basic principles and tools of the solution-oriented approach to companies in general and managers in particular. The learning effects of a solution-oriented approach can be used not only in appraisal interviews but in day-to-day management tasks.

The example of Solution Focused Rating has also been used to show that the classic management instruments can be designed from a solution-oriented perspective. Offering different management instruments appears to me to be one of the central challenges of solution management in the near future. These management tools (e.g. employee surveys, portfolios, balanced scorecard, etc.) are important 'possibility machines' (Jackson and McKergow 2002:70) and are still very problem-oriented. I believe that a major step towards further implementing the Solution Focused approach in companies will have been taken if it is possible to develop new and modified tools in this field within the next few years.

References

Bernardin, J, Kane J, Ross S, Spina J and Johnson D (1995), 'Performance Appraisal Design, Development, and Implementation', in: Ferris, R, Rosen S and Barnum, D (eds), *Handbook of Human Resource Management*, Cambridge, Blackwell.

Carrell, M, Elbert, N and Hatfield, R (1995), *Human Resource Management*, Englewood Cliffs, Prentice Hall.

Coens T and Jenkins, M (2002), *Abolishing Performance Appraisals*, San Francisco, Berret-Koehler Publications.

DeJong, P and Berg, I (1998), *Instructor's Resource Manual for Interviewing for Solutions*, Pacific Grove, Brooks Cole.

DeJong, P and Berg I (2002), *Interviewing for Solutions – 2nd edition*, Pacific Grove, Brooks Cole.

De Shazer, S (1997), *Putting Difference to Work*, Norton.

Jackson, P and McKergow, M (2002), *The Solutions Focus*, London, Nicholas Brealy.

Murphy, K (1996), *Understanding Performance Appraisal*, Thousand Oaks, Sage.

Biographical note

Dr. Günter Lueger is a management consultant and academic director of Coaching and Solution Management (the academic programme for Solution Management at the University of Management in Vienna, Austria). His innovations include management instruments like Misfit-Screening or Solution Focused Rating. He writes and trains in communication, performance management and change management.

Address: Pokornygasse 27/7, A-1190 Vienna, Austria.
E-mail: lueger@fit-management
Webpage: www.fit-management.at

Originally published in Organisations and People, Volume 10, Number 4, pages 34–40.

Organisational Constellations meets Appreciative Inquiry

Sue Abbotson and Patricia Lustig

A creative experiment in integrating two Organisational Transformation (OT) Disciplines

Introduction

Working separately in the field of organisational development for over fifteen years, we have been working together for the past few months on some exciting new possibilities for bringing together the emerging work of Organisational Constellations with the more well-known approach of Appreciative Inquiry (Ai). We want to share with you some of our thinking and excitement as to how these approaches can possibly support and enrich each other, whilst respecting the strengths they individually bring in their own right. Indeed it is our contention that only by recognising the power of the two approaches in their own right can we look for inter-connectedness without a loss of integrity of either approach.

One immediate difficulty in recounting the story of this inquiry is that there is so much to say about both approaches to convey the power and depth of their history and philosophical underpinning. For the sake of brevity we can only provide you with an overview of the essence of the approaches and how we see useful links between them. We assume that you will be more familiar with Ai and its benefits, but may be less familiar with Organisational Constellations and what these are, so we will spend more time explaining constellations. (If this is not the case, please look at our references.)

In brief, constellating is an approach to whole systems working which looks at the issues and dynamics of an organisation (or other system such as a family or community) using people as live representatives to provide feedback on the system. It bears some similarities to Moreno's psychodrama, except that crucially it looks at the consequences from the past, and works with hidden loyalties from the past as well as revealing the dynamics in the present. It can also work with the future in the present and point to resolving energies as well as bringing insights about the deep underlying, difficult issues that are holding a team or organisation back.

Constellations work from an epistemological basis that we are all part of an interconnected universe and thus can tap intuitively into an 'in-forming' or 'knowing' field using a level of knowledge beyond our rational or imaginative processes. It differs from the more humanistic Appreciative Inquiry which is a whole system engagement process designed to use the intuitive and creative possibilities of the system in a real time way. So why do we want to bring them together and possibly try to mix oil and water, when they stand so well alone?

The benefits of an integrated approach

One driver from the constellating perspective is that the constellation generates really powerful insights, but these are often done in the privacy of specialised constellation workshops where organisational leaders can work through their deep issues in a confidential setting. We want to make these powerful insights more available to the rest of the organisation. Indeed one Account Director we worked with on his relationship management issues told us 'You have given me the Enigma code, now all I need to do is crack them, to bomb the submarine.' You may not like the militaristic metaphor, but it does talk to the power of his experience and to a gap in 'where next ...'. As a constellator Sue was already aware of the importance of the three stages of the before, during and after of a constellation that could optimise the constellation in a transformational process. In short, some wider engagement process seemed necessary.

A driver from the Appreciative Inquiry perspective is the potential for the depth of insight that could really deepen and enrich the Discovery phase. Some of the beauty of Ai is in the appreciative discovery of heightened moments of what or when a system is working really well. Much can be done with this positive building momentum that takes people away from the moan and groan that can de-energise groups and foster secret or overt blaming and scapegoating. Whilst providing a positive platform for change that is owned, transparent and inclusive, the team in an Ai process may not face up to the deeper underlying patterns that can pull the organisational transformation off course, or lessen its impact. Starting with a constellation that points to the hidden issues, underlying patterns and unacknowledged realities of the system can fundamentally refine the focus of the Ai questions that start off the whole four-stage process.

Towards more sustainable transformation

If this is the story of how we have started to connect the potential for the processes, then our next step is to look deeper at how they can add value to an organisational journey of transformation. Like many other whole systems consultants, we have noticed that most change initiatives provide temporary improvements in situations, but that the underlying dynamics of the organisation remain the same. We also appreciate that some of the enduring qualities of an organisation clearly are beneficial; a compelling vision aligned with a sense of the founding purpose and a strong brand can provide coherence to the organisation that is more than a glue holding it together. There are however, underlying patterns of behaviour and meaning making as well as circumstantial and context issues that reduce the change agility of an organisation and, we have discovered, consume an energy that could be re-directed for transformation.

We think that organisations have an immense amount of energy, but are often caught in knotted patterns or 'entanglements' that prevent the healthy flow of this collective energy. Despite years of interventions the sum of the collective is not always more than the sum of its individual parts. There are usually pockets of excellence, individual heroes and moments of peak performance, but there is a collective sub-optimal performance. We are not interested in maximising one part of the system at the expense of the other, nor are we interested in moving the problem from one systemic element to the other in the appearance of making progress. Radical and sustainable transformation means re-constructing organisations in a way that makes it easier to deal with contradictions, opposites and multiple systems of thinking that we face in today's economic environment.

Our shared guiding principles for transformation

Bringing these approaches together requires us to think in terms of connecting operating principles. Some of these are:

- Working with analytical or verbal methods alone will not always work if we want to bring about deep-seated and sustainable change. Our normal way of knowing things in organisations and our normal beliefs about how we know things are much more limited than the intuitive knowledge that is actually available to us.
- We cannot undo behaviours of the past, but can acknowledge the consequences of what is and within these constraints make new choices.
- Our familiar stories that govern the leadership of change processes are only a partial truth, and not the way the system

is. Facing the hidden realities is a daunting task and needs a supportive change process that operates with integrity that goes beyond a loyalty to the commissioning client.

- Systemic behaviour can only be understood in its wider context and with new internal images of the future – new felt experiences – people are genuinely able to move away from their false loyalties based on covering hidden dynamics to co-creating tangible futures around their purpose.
- New behaviours will really make the difference and are often the simplest ways to bring about change, once people are free to behave in new ways.

What is organisational transformation?

As part of our co-inquiry into how can we bring about radical and transformative change in organisations we asked ourselves what 'form' it is that is being trans-formed in an organisational trans-form-ation. We believe that the 'form' that is undergoing a radical transformation of its parts into a new and greater whole, is the form of meaning making, how people view the organisation as a system and the resulting distribution of energies within the system. One of the critical insights from Bert Hellinger, who founded constellations in family systems, is that love doesn't just automatically 'flow' in the most beneficial way for all family members. He discovered that there is an architecture to the flow of love based on acknowledging everyone (including the forgotten or not-mentioned family members) in a system and including everyone through supporting them in finding their 'right' place. The resolved constellation provides a new internal image and a new felt experience for the issue holder, i.e. new (more compassionate) meanings which would continue to work, long after the completion of the constellation.

In organisational terms we have found that working with unconscious assumptions about the form, naming the taboos, acknowledging what isn't being said, or looking at the scapegoat as a doorway to an unspoken tension start to relax the system and release energy for change. For instance, in one constellation there was an apparent tension between a representative for profit and a representative for revenue. When revenue was moved to a new position, thus changing the spatial relationship between profit and revenue, we started to see a new relationship between them. A simple statement from revenue to profit, 'Revenue comes before profit' reinforced this change. The manager's insight was that his problems did not lie in his efforts around revenue or profit, but in the relationship between them. It seems so easy and clear after the insight, but had lain outside of his conscious awareness until that point. You can start to see how the discovery phase of the appreciative inquiry may be altered as a result of this insight. Ai with its emphasis on the intuitive dream phase and its more tangible collapse to form at the design and delivery phases then seems to add a consistent and yet different enough process to catalyse the deep insights of a constellation as a transformational tool.

Some working principles of constellating

Constellations and Ai are both action-orientated approaches in that they point to new actions and behaviours that will support change. A constellation starts with an interview identifying the really burning issues that occupy the issue holder in a system. The constellator most importantly listens to the issue without judgement, as no one is to blame for a series of inter-connected issues. The interviewer is thinking *relationally*, of hidden patterns and of consequences over time and does not want the detail of the familiar organisational story. Detachment from the issue holder is a vital skill at this point.

A constellation is set up by the issue holder using representatives – often people who know very little about the organisation. The client puts people who represent parts of their system in a space that represents the system. The client, or issue holder, will walk the various representatives to a place that feels comfortable. The representatives are asked to report on how they are feeling with regards

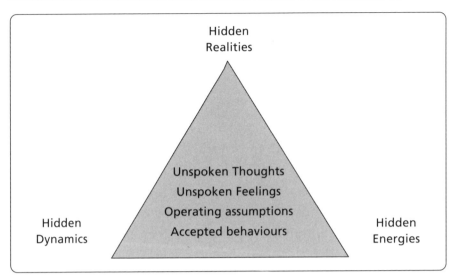

Figure 1

to other representatives. People are asked to focus on sensation and how their body feels, and to disengage thoughts and judgements. These sensations are usually uncannily accurate even though the representatives probably have no prior information about the system that they are representing.

As the constellation is set up it externalises the inner image that a client has of his or her system and represents it in three-dimensional space. It reveals the underlying dynamics that shape a system stripped of the details and points of view that lead to opinions and judgements. It reveals the hidden dynamics or the relationships between the things that make up the system. It also points to the hidden energies for change within the system, revealing where people would like to move and who seems to be holding tensions for the system or appears weighted down inappropriately.

To draw on a more rational, but possibly more familiar experience, a constellation is rather like using a spreadsheet where it is possible to see how changing one value will affect all others. You can move things in the system and see how the rest of the system responds to the change. In a constellation with an entrepreneur we looked at his issues with his Regional Development Agency and the local university and resolved some of the historical problems in their relationship. Turning to the future we saw that adding the 'customer' to his constellation improved the constellation, but adding 'prosperity' really brought it to life. People started to energise and to smile, shoulders dropped and you could feel the resolution. This entrepreneur changed his vision and his business plan as the result of the constellation. By slowly building the elements he could see both the critical dynamics that he needed to face and the complexity of the system that he had to work with.

Through this process of working with representative feedback, the constellation points to strains within the system and shows what might be possible within the given realities of a situation and where support might most economically and usefully be focussed so that change can take place. Experimental moves are made and sentences are given in the constellated system until a resolution is reached in which all members of the system have their appropriate place and feel more at peace. The constellator makes the experimental moves guided by the representative feedback and through stilling the mind and listening more to his or her intuitive or tacit knowing. It is simple, but not easy to do.

The moves include things like shifting people's position to make sure there are clear lines of vision, taking into account existing hierarchies, or re-including marginalised or excluded members. The moves help to establish a better flow of energy through the system by everyone having a place and being in their right place for the function they serve. The sentences are used to look into the hidden realities of the system and to resolve hidden dynamics. In a post-merger situation, for instance, it was important to use situations to acknowledge the difficulties of the merger discussions and the old loyalties to former organisations. Acknowledging 'what is' is often the critical intervention of a constellation. We can then release energy for new possibilities and new internal images of the system.

Appreciative Inquiry

For Appreciative Inquiry to be effective, it is important that all the relevant PEOPLE are in the room for the inquiry: those who are responsible and needed to make the change happen. The appreciative inquiry finds the energy for change in an organisation based on what has worked well for the organisation in the past and helping to move that into the present.

We begin by Discovering our strengths in areas where we have had success in the past. Using what we have discovered as 'resources', we ask the team to consider what else they could build based upon those wonderful resources. It makes sense, after all, to build upon what works, rather than what doesn't. This is called the Dream Phase and we focus on the best of what could be. We build on the energy and use it to create new possibilities together.

The next part is the Design Phase where the group decides which part of their dream they want to make happen and in what order. This is a time of negotiation between people, most especially around

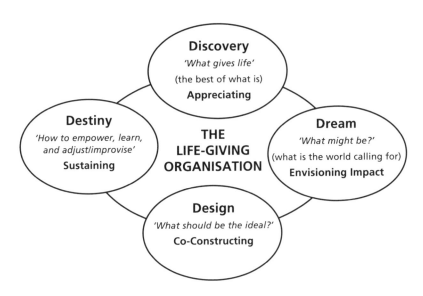

Figure 2

how they can support one another. At this stage we may need to draw upon more traditional consultancy methods such as performance metrics to identify the new capabilities and design how they will be developed. Creating communities of practice can be one very good process for continuing the inquiry at this stage. The final part is the Delivery Phase where each individual who wishes to, stands up and commits to do his or her part of what was to happen. This leads to the next steps and further opportunities for reinforcing the insights from the original constellation, or if necessary conducting further focused constellations as the organisation progresses with the change process.

Insight led transformation – the key to deeper more enduring change

We have already acknowledged that there are strong separate uses for both of these approaches, and indeed are aware of other transformational techniques such as systemic coaching to leverage the insights from a constellation. Increasingly as constellations are starting to take place within organisations and a leader needs to move forward with the insight from the constellation as part of a wider organisational transformation, we believe that designing an appreciative inquiry to focus the new energy for change within the organisation is an extremely effective method to use.

The first step we have pointed to in this integrated approach is to use a constellation to provide a depth of insight into a change process. The wisdom of the constellation is working with the 'below the radar' issues and acknowledging what really cannot be changed. Participants see key movements within a constellation, which point towards next steps, and occasionally reveal very clear decisions that need to be made. Sustaining the deep insights is the next step. This helps us to see where we need to focus the appreciative inquiry as a way of bringing the wider system together around these new insights. A whole system engagement process can then really add value with integrating the change process. We feel that Ai is an especially appropriate process because the depth of insight from having participated in the constellation gives a person a very positive impetus for change. We believe that the Ai will be more successful as a result of the deeper starting point and with the released energy from the old loyalties and old patterns of behaving. Our next step is testing and refining the best combinations of these approaches in relation to client needs. We hope that we have found a way of combining field and systems thinking in a positive and appreciative way that will enable a client organisation to transform in a largely self managed way, and that will enable it to develop the most appropriate capabilities for moving forward with its own vision and purpose and really strengthen their place in the market in a sustainable way.

An emerging case study

Sue was asked by a Talent team leader to constellate an issue around the relationship of Talent to HR in a changing business environment. This was an in-house constellation and so required sensitivity to the power and trust issues that were present. In such an case it is often better to offer an insight constellation, which gives new insights about a situation, as opposed to a resolution constellation which points to a resolution that suits all the stakeholders, as this may involve facing more than a team new to constellations in a work environment are ready to face. Clearly, contracting around the expectations is critical.

Two representatives for Talent and HR were set up. The first striking thing about the representatives was that they were all facing the same direction. They were asked what were they looking at, and all agreed it was the future of the business. This was also represented, which changed things. The Talent representatives felt small in relation to HR. The HR representatives on the other hand split with one feeling very powerful and police-like, whilst the other felt more interested in the Talent. As the constellation progressed the Talent team seemed to want to stay loyal to values such as trust as honesty, whereas HR were happier with business values. The wider business was also added and Talent reported being torn between wanting to move closer to the business and staying near HR. Business also lost interest when Talent and HR seemed more interested in the issues between them than in the business issues.

As an insight constellation, the Talent team felt that this was an important piece of work, pointing to the need to clarify their identity, their business model, their relationship assets and their values. Until this point they were locked into "it isn't fair what HR are doing", and couldn't see a route to action. There appears to be a need for some strategising work in terms of how they can move closer to the business as partners rather than suppliers. They may also require work on business fluency and language, so that they seem "less innocent" than the constellation was revealing.

One way that we could move forward is around an inquiry that looks at times when there has been a very clear sense of identity for the unit and this means times when they have partnered well. People were not totally clear about what they meant by partnering and understanding and clarifying this will help people to do it better. To do this, we can ask:

- Tell us a story about a time when you experienced an excellent partnering relationship with HR. What happened? What were you doing? How did it feel? How did others react?
- Tell us about a time when you experienced an excellent partnering relationship with the business. What happened? What did you do? How did it make you (and others) feel? How did others react?
- What were the differences? The similarities?

Using what we discover from these questions we can build new ways for people to work that incorporate the best of both partnership relationships and helps to strengthen the team identity, their alignment and their ability to partner with other parts of the organisation.

References

For more about organisational and family constellations:

http://www.nowherefoundation.org

http://www.hellinger.com

For more about Appreciative Inquiry visit:

The Appreciative Inquiry Commons run by Case Western Reserve University

http://www.appreciativeinquiry.cwru.edu

http://www.lasadev.com

Biographical note

Sue Abbotson PhD is an organisational constellator and whole system transformation consultant. For the past two years she has been working as a researcher and practitioner for the nowherefoundation. Her focus has been on leading the integration of organisational constellations with wider transformation processes. She also works as a systemic coach supporting the resolution of organisational constellations. She is a member of the teaching faculty in the Fundamentals of Organisational Constellations and Learning Forums over the coming year. In addition to this, Sue works a senior consultant at Bath Consultancy Group where she is currently working with the application of constellations in strategic account management for the financial and professional services sectors. Previous experience includes lecturing in the Management of Innovation at the University of Bath and researching into Creativity, Executive Learning and Leadership.

Patricia Lustig is Managing Director of LASA Development UK Ltd. an international consultancy group. She works at all levels and has exceptional experience with understanding of European and Asian cultures where she advises national and international organisations, both in the profit and the not-for-profit sector. She specialises in the use of Appreciative Inquiry (Ai) as a change methodology and is particularly interested in developing the next generation of Ai practice, linking Ai into the creative process. She is a Member of the IOD and a Founder Member of UKCLC. She is also an Associate of Bath Consultancy Group and a member of the nowherecommunity.

Originally published in Organisations and People, Volume 10, Number 4, pages 41–48.

Solution Focused Strategic Planning

Jim Mortensen

Can a solutions focus enhance the venerable processes of strategic planning? Jim Mortensen tries it out and gets some feedback from experienced planning facilitators in the US Government.

As strategic planners, too many of us have heard the groans of participants as we start our planning sessions. Employees sabotage the effort. Even comic strips lampoon the process. And all too often, the best developed plans seem to break apart in the implementation phase.

One effective resolution to this issue can be found in applying principles that have coalesced together from the fields of communications, complexity theory and therapy. This approach to positive change is called the Solutions Focus (SF). In this article I will present a few ideas for improving the strategic planning process through the use of SF techniques.

A quick overview of strategic planning

Most of us are familiar with strategic planning. If we have not facilitated a planning session, then we probably have suffered through one. It is the process wherein an organisation identifies its purpose and goals, develops a vision of itself in the future and then defines a course of action to reach that desired future (Donald, Lyons and Tribbey, 2001). The process also identifies the participants and

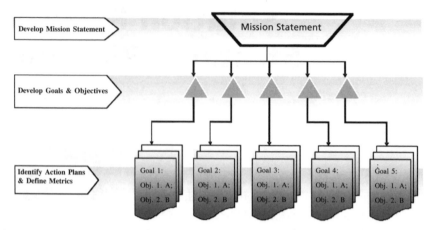

Figure 1 – Schematic of the Strategic Planning Process

resources necessary to carry the plan to fruition. The focal point of strategic planning is the future repercussions of current choices (Bryson, 1988).

To facilitate the creation of an effective plan, many facilitators tend use the following building blocks (See Figure 1 for the standard Strategic Plan outline):

- SWOT Analyses (Strengths, Weaknesses, Opportunities and Threats).
- Vision and mission statements.
- Strategic goals and objectives.
- Action plans and evaluation metrics.

Using this process we planning facilitators lead our groups from looking at where the organisation is now, to where it should be in the future, and then how to get there. We try to keep our work results-oriented, making sure that goals and objectives are 'objective, quantifiable, and measurable' (GPRA, Sec. 4 (b)).

How effective is it?

Though there is general agreement regarding the importance of strategic planning, researches have not uncovered much in the way of benefits. Capon, Farley and Hulbert (1994) found there was a clear though small benefit from strategic planning. However, in a recent review of efficacy studies, Phillips and Moutinho (2000) reported mixed results. In general, they note that many firms gain no benefit from strategic planning and in those that do, the gains are limited. So, though the case for strategic planning would seem to be self-evident, something additional is needed to increase its effectiveness.

What would be a useful facilitation model for strategic planning?

One researcher points incisively to where a real deficit exists. In 1994, Mintzberg suggested that the focus has been too much on the formal top-down development of the strategic plan and not enough on making it a part of the company. He advocates that planners be trained to creatively identify existing strategic initiatives within an organisation. He says that planners' intent should be 'to pose the right questions rather than to find the right answers' (Mintzberg, 1994:112). Strategic planners should not be the experts in programming strategy so much as the facilitators of its development. Their purpose should be to foster a positive vision of the future and then to lead the search to find innovative solutions within the organisation. Given the importance these researchers confer to the facilitators, it is surprising that there is such a lack of research into effective facilitation models specific to strategic planning. As planners and consultants, we each have a portfolio of preferred facilitation activities. But if we are asked to describe the theory behind the practice, it might be difficult to articulate a coherent philosophy directly related to strategic planning.

Since current planning research proffers little in the area of facilitation methodologies, it makes sense to turn to a field that focuses on change facilitation models – namely the field of therapy. One model of therapy that is gaining increasing credibility is Solution Focused Brief Therapy (SFBT). The similarities between Mintzberg's vision of strategic planning and SFBT are striking. The purpose of SFBT is to help clients develop a vision of a preferred state and then to assist them in utilising their current resources to accomplish this vision. A couple of pioneers in the Solution Focused field, Bill O'Hanlon and Michelle Weiner-Davis, describe SFBT as a process wherein the client envisions a future free of the identified problems, and the therapist subsequently facilitates the client's definition and clarification of the desired end-state, making it behavioural, and breaking it down into small, manageable steps. It is SFBT's emphasis on measurable steps and attainable goals which appears to provide a potential solution to some of strategic planning's shortcomings.

How does SF fit with strategic planning?

A Solutions Focus is based on the following principles:

- An emphasis on what is going well.
- Utilisation of existing resources and processes.
- A belief in the client as the expert.
- Simplicity.
- The inevitability of change.
- A present and future orientation.
- Co-operation.
- Replication of existing successful strategies.
- Replacement of unsuccessful strategies.

SFBT seeks to move 'away from explanations [and] problems ... and towards solutions, competence, and capabilities' (O'Hanlon and Weiner-Davis, 1989:6). It is far less concerned about how problems developed than it is with how they will be solved. Imagine a strategic planning session where everyone focused on forward-looking possibilities not where things went wrong.

In 2002, Cauffman and Berg discussed the use of a Solutions Focus in corporate coaching. They noted that many strategy sessions within a business descend into meetings that are demoralising and focused on obstacles. Solution Focused coaching, on the other hand, shifts both the tone and the focus of strategy sessions to a positive, resolution orientation (Cauffman and Berg, 2002). The authors suggest implementing SF techniques, such as the *Miracle Question*, for resolving a number of corporate issues, including mergers, inter-departmental conflict, disputes in family-owned businesses, etc.

In April 2002, Jackson and McKergow published *The Solutions Focus*. The book provides a case study discussing the use of a Solution Focused approach in strategic planning for a non-profit film institute in Canada. In the institute's strategic planning offsite, the Glasgow Group focused on organisational strengths as a foundation for the company's future (Glasgow Group, 2002). *Exception-Finding Questions* were used to identify moments of success in prior chaotic situations. *Miracle* and *Scaling Questions* were used to develop descriptive action plans for the future. When there was a gap noted between current skills and future needs, the question was asked 'When this is no longer an issue/problem, what will we be doing?'. Participants' responses were built into the planning. The Glasgow Group credits their Solutions Focused approach with an increase in team cohesion and greater organisational alignment.

What are some useful SF techniques for strategic planning?

By nature, a Solutions Focus fosters a collaborative relationship between the facilitator and the client. Using a non-confrontational approach, in-house facilitators avoid conflict with senior executives who may also be in their direct chain of command. Based on co-operative Solutions Focused principles, practitioners have developed a number of techniques.

Getting participant buy-in

Participant buy-in is critical to the strategic planning process. Too often there are naysayers to the process. It is important to bring these people into the process, even though they may be 'resistant', 'uncooperative', and 'often hostile' (De Jong and Berg, 2001:361). Otherwise the whole planning process gets hi-jacked by one or two individuals.

Attempting to coerce or argue with a naysayer is usually a lose-lose proposition. Instead, a solutions-focused entrée would be to identify what he or she might actually be a customer for. It may be necessary to explore the complainant's concerns in more detail to find an area where the complainant *is* interested in taking some ownership of the process (Berg and Miller, 1992). The time invested upfront is well worth the payoff of lower conflict and better information.

A Solutions Focus provides the important framework that the criticisms offered may in fact be credible and the information provided could be useful in developing more effective strategic plans. The role of client-as-expert is pivotal in the Solution Focused approach. Rather than manipulating complainant-type participants into compliance, the SF facilitator seeks for their assistance in co-creating solutions. Solution Focused practitioners tend to view a client's resistance as the client's assistance in noting roadblocks and identifying more useful approaches.

Hearing and empathising with the client accomplishes two things. First, it gathers useful information about the process. Second, it works to invite the client into the process as opposed to mandated participation which Mintzberg (1994) describes as 'calculating'. He further states that 'strategies take on value only as committed people infuse them with energy' (p. 109). Thus a Solutions Focus, where the client is heard and respected, may prove particularly useful in planning sessions where participation is mandated.

Using coping questions

Often complainants argue that nothing changes, and that *this* strategic planning effort will be no different (Franklin, 2001). *Coping Questions* can help elicit co-operative feedback from people who doubt the efficacy of strategic planning.

Coping Questions start with a hearing-out of the complainant's concerns. Listening closely is important as it allows the facilitator to understand the complainant better and later more effectively to co-create solutions wherein the complainant actively desires to contribute (Berg and Miller, 1992).

In an organisational setting, individuals may affix the failure of past initiatives on the lack of support or interference from higher authorities in the bureaucracy. Some responsive *Coping Questions* to this 'passing the buck' might include:

- How have you continued to lead in this organisation even with this type of oversight?
- What are some of the ways you have managed to work around the interference?
- What are some of the ways this planning session can help you do more of what you're already accomplishing?

These questions acknowledge the challenges that team members have encountered in previous efforts, while also recognising that they *have* made progress *despite* the obstacles. The purpose of asking these Coping Questions is to hear the complainant, collect useful information, and to co-create a solution in which they have ownership.

Miracle questions

A useful technique for developing mission/vision statements and for strategic goal setting is to use *Miracle Questions*. A common *Miracle Question* adapted to strategic planning might be 'If a miracle happened and you came to work tomorrow morning and this organisation was everything you described in your vision statement, what will be different?'

Possible follow-up questions include:

- Are there small pieces of this that are already occurring?
- What do you need to do to make it happen more?
- How will your job be different?

- Which of the organisation's constituencies will be among the first to notice?
- What will they notice?
- How will they respond?

The facilitator continues to ask these questions to make the vision rich, 'vivid and concrete' (De Jong and Berg, 2001:370).

Miracle Questions also help to clarify goals. By using this process, the facilitator has helped the session's participants to identify a conceptual target as their strategic goal. Used in conjunction with *Scaling Questions* (see section below), the facilitator could also help executives create numerical targets for the purpose of evaluating their progress. These questions can be combined with *Action Descriptions* to make the mission and vision statements more concrete.

Action descriptions

When a facilitator is helping participants to development *Action Descriptions* she requires clients to describe in concrete terms how their mission statements translate into everyday actions. These descriptions provide the groundwork for developing action plans and metrics. An activity that encourages the development of *Action Descriptions* would emphasise the *who, what, when, where,* and *how* that are critical to effective action plans.

Exception-finding questions

Often, a focus on failure can lead to in-fighting and finger pointing. Yet, usually clients are already having some success towards their goals. The fact that any organisation currently exists is evidence that it did something successfully at some previous time. By working with team members to identify those success stories, they may see possible strategies to implement and to expand upon. Identifying past organisational successes creates the possibility for future successes. Potential discussion questions include:

- What progress towards its goals is the organisation currently making?
- What successes has this organisation had in the past?
- Who have been past leaders when the organisation had these successes?
- What did these leaders do to contribute to the successes?
- How did the workforce contribute?
- How did the leadership engage the workforce?
- Who else contributed to the successes?
- What did they do?
- How did they initially buy in to the effort?
- Who outside the organisation noticed the success?
- What parts of the success did they notice?

The answers to these questions will provide methods and actions that can be implemented to accomplish the current goals. Such questions also emphasise the potential for future successes.

Scaling questions

Using *Scaling Questions* in strategic planning may help the planning group break the action plans down into manageable pieces. With *Scaling Questions*, clients place their current progress on a scale, usually using 1 and 10 as their anchors, with the company's vision as a 10 and total failure as a 1. Once they have identified their current state and had the opportunity to discuss their subjective measurement, they would then be asked what it would take to move them up a point on the scale, e.g. from 5 to 6, or an even smaller increment such as a 5.1 to a 5.2.

To further leverage the utility of *Scaling Questions*, the management team could also be asked to evaluate the organisation from the perspectives of key stakeholders, such as the workforce, the customers, or others in the chain-of-command. Giving strategic planners the opportunity to take these additional perspectives serves a dual purpose. It provides management a reality check for their goals; and it helps them design their action plans to have maximum impact across stakeholder groups.

Evaluation

The focus of strategic planning is on creating successful results. In order to measure success, it is necessary to implement measurement steps and to evaluate progress on a continual basis. Measurement metrics need to be quantifiable. In a Solutions Focus approach, the evaluation phase is used to highlight the progress that has been made and to keep the client focused on the positive (Berg and Miller, 1992).

The natural tendency will be to look at how far short of the goal a team or manager has fallen in the measurement of their accomplishments. However, by looking at the chain of events and elements that led to goal attainment as envisioned in the strategic plan, planners will have identified successful processes for replication in future iterations.

Results of the Study

Most managers are rightfully sceptical of new management techniques, so I tested the process with a group of highly experienced planners that worked for a large agency. I chose government planners because they tend to be more sceptical of consultants than most businesses. The test group consisted of six planners with an average of 13.7 years facilitation experience. In the study, the planners were presented the Solutions Focus model, were given a three hours training block in its use, and were then given an opportunity to provide quantitative and qualitative feedback on how useful Solutions Focus techniques would be in their work. The results lead to several interesting findings.

During the post-training evaluation, participants were given a matrix of strategic planning activities and SF techniques. See the table below for the matrix results. The planners were then asked to match which techniques they would use for each of the planning stages.

Table. Frequency Counts of Participant Matches for SF Technique to Appropriate Strategic Planning Stage

PLANNING STAGE	SOLUTION FOCUSED TECHNIQUES				
	Coping Questions	Miracle Questions	Action Descriptions	Exception-Finding Questions	Scaling Questions
Developing A Mission Statement	3	5	2		1
Setting Strategic Goals And Objectives	3	5	4	4	5
Designing Action Plans	2	1	6	4	4
Defining Milestones	1	1	6	3	3

Cells shaded indicate a majority of respondents selected the technique indicated in that column for use with the planning stage indicated in that row. For example, five people indicated they would use Miracle Questions when Developing a Mission Statement.

Participants specified that they would use *Miracle Questions* for strategic level stages such as Developing a Mission Statement and Setting Strategic Goals. However, there was a drop in support for using *Miracle Questions* in later stages. *Action Descriptions* proved to be the most selected tool for these more detailed planning stages.

There was strong support for using *Scaling Questions* when Setting Strategic Goals and Objectives but not for developing metrics. This was a surprise, since *Scaling Questions* seem to be a good fit for measuring progress.

A significant problem in many strategic plans is linking broader goals with action planning. Perhaps for this reason, study participants were eager to try almost all of the SF techniques when facilitating these middle phases. In addition, a majority of respondents selected *Action Descriptions* across three of the planning stages. The use of *Action Descriptions* through several stages of the planning bodes well for creating a continuous linkage from one phase to the next. If facilitators use the Solutions Focused techniques across phases as they indicated, there will be a natural connection between the mission statement, the goals, and the action plans to support those goals.

The only match not to receive a vote was the use of *Exception-Finding Questions* with Developing a Mission Statement. The specific focus of this technique versus the global nature of mission statements make this an improbable match.

Respondents were also given the opportunity to make any additional comments they wanted. There was unambiguous support for using a Solution Focused approach in a corporate setting beyond strategic planning. The common theme was the benefits of a Solutions Focus on well-defined end-states and on developing the map with clear actions for achieving the stated goals.

According to the participants, the positive nature of a Solutions Focus encourages a productive tone in team meetings. It was stated in both the survey instrument and in a follow-up group discussion session that Solutions Focused techniques would be useful in bringing critics into the planning process. A weakness that was mentioned was the terminology. Participants were concerned that therapy vocabulary as well as terms such as 'miracle' could be a potential hindrance when working with senior executives. Respondents suggested adapting the vocabulary to the organisation's culture.

This study was a helpful confirmation that a Solutions Focus approach can be helpful in corporate planning sessions. Participants liked the additional tools it provided, the positive mindset and the co-operative approach. They indicated that the forward-looking orientation of SF fosters a productive atmosphere for team meetings, noting that a Solutions Focus tends to side-step destructive confrontations while still addressing the pertinent issues of the organisation.

Conclusion

In summary, a Solutions Focus is about enhancing success – not in new, proprietary methodologies, but in simple, concrete steps. Strategic planning offers great potential to organisations, but there is still a great deal of room for improvement. Some of this improvement can come by changing strategic plans from stale PowerPoint presentations to living embodiments of the company's successes. A Solutions Focus does this by using principles and tools that engage managers in connecting the plan with the workforce's actual contributions.

References

Berg, IK, and Miller, SD (1992), *Working with the Problem Drinker*, New York, WW Norton & Company, Inc.

Bryson, JM (1988), *Strategic Planning for Public and Non-profit Organizations: A Guide to Strengthening and Sustaining Organizational Achievement*, Jossey-Bass, San Francisco.

Capon, N, Farley, JU and Hulbert, JM (1994), 'Strategic planning and financial performance: More evidence', *The Journal of Management Studies, 31*, 105–110, Oxford. Abstract from: ABI/Inform.

Cauffman, L, and Berg, IK (2002), 'Solution Focused Corporate Coaching', *LERNENDE ORGANISATION*, Jänner/Februar 2002. English translation retrieved July 12, 2002 from http://www.solution-focused-management.com/en/inhoud/SolFoc.doc.

De Jong, P, and Berg, IK (2001), 'Co-constructing cooperation with mandated clients', *Social Work*, Vol. 46 No. 4, 361–374.

Donald, CG, Lyons, TS, and Tribbey, RC (2001), 'A partnership for strategic planning and management in a public organization', *Public Performance and Management Review, 25*, 176–193, Sage Publications.

Franklin, AL (2001), 'Serving the public interest? Federal experiences with participation in strategic planning', *American Review Of Public Administration, 31* (2), 126–138, Sage Publications, Inc.

Glasgow Group (2002), *Using the Solution Focus approach the Toronto International Film Festival transforms itself into a strategically driven business*, Downloaded July 15, 2002 from http://www.glasgrp.com/main.asp?SubSection=strategic_planning.

Government Performance and Results Act of 1993, Pub. L. No. 103–62.

Mintzberg, H (1994), 'The fall and rise of strategic planning', *Harvard Business Review*, January–February, 107–114.

O'Hanlon, WH, and Weiner-Davis, M (1989), *In Search of Solutions*, New York, WW Norton & Company, Inc.

Phillips, PA and Moutinho, L (2000), 'The strategic planning index: a tool for measuring strategic planning effectiveness', *Journal of Travel Research*, 38, 369–379, Sage Publications.

Biographical note

Jim's background is in systems intervention, both at the organisational and the small team level. He has worked as a consultant to the US federal government in organisational development and strategic planning. Jim completed his thesis on the use of Solution Focused techniques in strategic planning. He has a Masters of Science in human development from Virginia Tech and is currently pursuing a Masters in Public Administration at Brigham Young University. His research interests include organisational development in corporate, public and non-profit organisations as well as sustainable development in developing countries. He can be reached at jim_mortensen@yahoo.com.

Originally published in Organisations and People, Volume 10, Number 4, pages 49–57.

Making Competency Management Work:

Use What is There!

Gwenda Schlundt Bodien and Coert Visser

Devising a system of management competencies is all very well, but as a consultant how can you achieve this while staying both solutions focused and client directed? Coert Visser and Gwenda Schlundt Bodien report on their experiences.

The challenge of making competency management work

We were asked by a large Dutch governmental organisation to manage a competency management project, based on our expertise in this field. We knew that whilst many organisations put a lot of effort into developing these kinds of systems, the system often became an end in itself. We did not want this. Our challenge was to make competency management really work within this organisation. We were convinced that the Solution Focused approach could be of great help so we decided to apply Solution Focused principles in the process of developing competency management.

What is competency management?

First a few words on competency management – a big thing in the world of Dutch governmental organisations. Basically it consists of a set of instruments describing what competencies are required in a certain job and how these competencies might be developed. Its goals are:

- To talk about HOW people do their work, as well as WHAT they do
- To improve people's effective work behaviour
- To focus personal, team and organisational development
- To improve business results
- To have an integrated set of HR policies and systems

Our goal: teaching the client to fish

The governmental organisation asked us to develop a competency system for the entire organisation. This implied managing the project, developing the competencies and the competency profiles for distinctive jobs and implementing the new systems so that they would contribute to the performance of the organisation. We had been introduced to the Solution Focused approach a few years earlier and were convinced of the value of the approach. Managing a competency management project sounded like an assignment in which our HR expertise was most important to the client; however we were eager to apply the Solution Focused approach and shift away from 'Expertise Input'. We saw our focus as facilitating the process and teaching the clients to build their own solutions. To use a metaphor: we were not providing the client with fish, we were teaching the clients to fish themselves.

The Solution Focused approach

A few words now on what struck us about the Solution Focused approach. Two features of the Solution Focus are important to mention:

The strengths perspective: Users of the Solution Focused approach find it more useful to focus attention directly on building solutions for problems than on analysing causes of problems and making a diagnosis.

Inductive approach: The Solution Focused consultant does not usually provide generic theory-based advice but helps his/her clients discover and develop their own solutions that fit their unique circumstances. The Solution Focused consultant often employs a so-called 'Not Knowing' attitude.

In practice the Solution Focused approach comes down to:

1. **Acknowledging problems**: first of all acknowledge the problem you might have. In what sense is it a problem? How does it bother you?
2. **Defining the preferred future**: specify how you would like things to be
3. **Identifing solutions**: identify what helps you make progress in that desired direction (find out what works)
4. **Amplifying solutions**: if something works, do MORE of it

If you notice something does not work, stop doing it and do something ELSE (Visser and Schlundt Bodien, 2002)

We summarise the basic principles of the solutions focused approach with the following acronym (Visser and Schlundt Bodien, 2003):

P – problems are acknowledged but NOT analysed,
O – outcomes desired are specified,
W– where are you now on the scale?
E – exceptions to the problem are keys to solutions,
R – relationships are enhanced and made productive,
S – small steps forward lead to larger change.

The project

During the project we kept asking ourselves several questions, two of which seemed particularly important. The first question was:

1. How to make competency management Solution Focused?

We started the competency management project by interviewing all members of the management team individually. We asked them a very Solution Focused question:

'Suppose you are a year further down the line and competency management really contributes to the performance of your department, what would you see happening in the day-to-day work?'

This question turned out to be very useful. The answers varied a lot, as might be expected, but in essence the ultimate goal boiled down to 'getting the work done well'. The organisation had just gone through a period of efficiency improvements and were now working towards improving the quality of their services and work processes.

Not only did the Solution Focus prove helpful for facilitating the *process* of the competency management project, it also proved very useful regarding the *content*. The following content issues were all inspired by the Solution Focus – the suggestions being welcomed enthusiastically by our client because they fitted well with their overall project goal.

Take a strengths perspective: What is going well? What competencies do you already show? 80% of the appraisal conversation should be about strengths and successes (see Visser and Thissen, 2002) and build competencies on what is already there. Focus on maximising competencies that are there, instead of minimising deficiencies. Don't let competency management stop employees doing what they are already doing well.

Use a tailored approach: Avoid forcing generic solutions on people. Each individual gives his/her own flavour to a competency; allow and encourage individualised solutions.

Use an interactional perspective: Use competencies that facilitate interaction and co-operation between people.

Be goal-oriented: Competency management is a means to an end, not an end in itself. Make sure that through competency management, individuals and teams can achieve what is really important for them.

Use the development perspective: The Solution Focus is aimed at helping people make progress in the direction of their choice, not on making judgements and measurements. That is why we suggested focusing on development instead of focusing on measurement and rewards.

The second question we dealt with was:

2. How to stay client directed?
Until recently we had been applying the Solution Focus mainly with individuals and small groups, but now we faced a large and complex organisation. We wrestled with the following question: Who exactly IS the client in a complex conflicting organisation? How deeply can/should we go into the content and into the organ-

isation? How do we stay client directed? How do we avoid the temptations of taking the lead (instead of following the client) and applying our own expertise (instead of taking a Not-Knowing attitude).

In our project team, we often discussed and grappled with the complex issue of staying as much 'at the surface' of the organisation as possible, whilst still offering our expertise as appropriate. Some of the actions regarding these issues that we found helpful were:

Finding common goals, however small. Sometimes interests and goals seem to be so much in conflict that we were about to choose sides. But every single time the question 'What do we all agree about?' proved that there were more common points of view and common interests than there were conflicting ones. It is often a matter of focusing on common interests and common goals, however small, and building from there.

Letting less-involved people off the hook: Not every single manager was fully interested in competency management. Instead of fighting this attitude and trying to convince these managers that they ought to be supporting the project, we deliberately helped them to be as 'little bothered' as possible. From those at the other end of the Project Interest Scale, we formed a users group made up of a number of decision-making managers who had most to gain from competency management and its implementation. These managers regarded the competency management project as a means of knowing what the other managers were involved with. Involving the managers who had something to gain and not bothering the ones who weren't interested worked well.

Bringing the management team together and letting them take the lead. Before every management team meeting at which we were present, each manager was individually asked 'What should take place in the meeting in order for you to feel it was worth your time?'. This pre-meeting questioning enabled managers to ensure that, during the meetings, they raised the themes that they wanted to discuss and we could ask them how they wanted to deal with the issues. This approach helped this management team to come up with their own answers through their own thought processes.

Trusting the client and loving confusion: Sometimes there was so much going on during the management team meetings or in the whole organisation for that matter that we were all utterly confused as to what our next step should be. We learned to trust the client and to love the confusion ... Confusion serves a purpose; it keeps everybody awake and at a certain point there is someone taking the lead and speaking the freeing words that everybody agrees on. Confusion helps the client to find his or her own solutions – our role as consultants is merely to facilitate that process.

Context expertise is allowed

The project is still in full operation. The results are good. Employees throughout the organisation have been involved in developing an organisation-wide competency system. This employee involvement helps them to see how competency management could be of use to them. The Solution Focused approach helped us to really help our client do what they wanted to do. It prevented us from imposing any expert-driven solutions on them but it also helped us to identify situations in which our team of consultants DID have to use our competency management expertise. A not-knowing attitude was very often helpful, but sometimes expertise was required. This last point is quite interesting, because we found that adding expertise is only necessary when the client lets us know that they are stuck because of a lack of specific knowledge. In that case, providing the client with your expertise is a very Solution Focused thing to do.

Concluding remarks

Even today, the authors, as consultants, continue to discuss with each other the issues addressed in this article. It makes our work much more interesting ... we help each other not to become solution forced; which means that we try to lead from behind, following the client in their wishes and never specifically talking about the Solutions Focused approach as such. We simply apply the principles ourselves and if the client becomes curious as to where these strange questions come from we are happy to share our knowledge of how SF works and what we believe in.

And, yes, we still believe in the Solutions Focused approach! At times everything seems to go wrong and nothing seems to work out right. When that happens we look at each other in despair and ask ourselves 'Does the Solutions Focused approach really work, or have we come across such a complicated situation that we must admit that it doesn't work any more?'

So far, we still come up with the same answer: 'The Solution Focused approach works perfectly fine as long as we keep on applying it!'

References

De Jong, Peter and Insoo Kim Berg (2001), *Interviewing for solutions*, Wadsworth Publishing.

Jackson, Paul Z and McKergow, Mark (2002), *The Solutions Focus: The SIMPLE Way to Positive Change*, Nicholas Brealey.

Visser, Coert and Schlundt Bodien, Gwenda (2003), *The POWERS of the solution focus*, www.hr.com.

Visser, Coert and Schlundt Bodien, Gwenda (2003), *Solution focused coaching: simply effective*, www.hr.com.

Visser, Coert and Thissen, Maarten (2002), *Effective Managers Pay Attention to Strengths*, www.hr.com.

Biographical note

Gwenda Schlundt Bodien (gsb.positron@planet.nl) and Coert Visser (coert.visser@planet.nl) are self-employed management consultants and coaches living in the Netherlands. They are members of The Competency Network (the team of consultants that carried out the project described in this case). Coert and Gwenda founded the Dutch Network of Solution Focused consultants and managers, NOAM and have written several articles on the Solution Focus.

Originally published in Organisations and People, Volume 10, Number 4, pages 58–62.

Solution Focused Feedback in Management Development

Dr. Peter Röhrig

This article features ideas about the value of SF conversations using criticism and praise as well as detailed instructions about a training exercise to help people learn how to give effective criticism. It is partly directed to managers about the value of SF conversations and partly to trainers about a training exercise in SF conversations. The exercise works on more than one level: the volunteer has the opportunity to practise a real situation and at the same time all the other participants get the chance to practise their skills by giving feedback to him.

What works well already?

Every boss knows how difficult it is to criticise colleagues constructively. Before sharing some suggestions for trying out something different in your role as a supervisor or trainer, I would like to ask you to think about the following question:

How have you already succeeded in criticising someone in a way that he or she has accepted without being hurt or insulted i.e. where the criticism had the consequences you hoped for?

Please put aside this article for one moment to think about such a situation – it does not matter whether it is in your occupational or private life – and try to remember as much detail and be as concrete as possible. What was it that made you criticise successfully? What did you do, through good preparation, choice of words, patience or what else? What did your counterpart contribute? Which (possibly lucky) circumstances were helpful?

With this small 'thought experiment' you have already set the foundation for better feedback behaviour. You realised your resources and positive experiences. This is a basic principle of Solution Focused work, which you can use in many situations. You will find starting points for individual solutions by focusing on positive experiences instead of problems.

Positive feedback

You can praise yourself now for this successful experience and thereby strengthen your feedback behaviour; you should also praise your colleagues whenever it is appropriate to the situation. You could possibly do that more frequently than you may imagine. The most common complaint colleagues have about their bosses is 'I do not receive enough acknowledgement for my work!' As supervisors we tend to talk to colleagues when something is going wrong. If everything runs fine, we are content and keep our satisfaction to ourselves.

You can easily change that. Start to pay attention to situations in your everyday work life, in which colleagues do something which is helpful to you and your business and which you have so far accepted as 'normal'. Whether this is the skilful handling of a difficult customer or the clear and complete decision plan prepared for you, invest in that moment so that you can give your colleagues the acknowledgement they deserve for doing well. You can be sure that you will improve their motivation with appropriate praise.

Praise is appropriate when it is open and honest, clear and without reservation as well as relevant to the situation. With some practice you can extend the praise by Solution Focused questions (Schmitz 2000:21). For example, ask more frequently about 'How did you do that?' when you have an honest interest in the answer.

For instance: 'You had that good suggestion about recommendations from our regular customers. How did you come up with that?'

Open criticism by your colleagues is usually an indication that you have created a fearless atmosphere and that your colleagues feel that you are interested in their opinions. You might invite comment by saying 'I am very glad that we made the contract in such a short time. How do you feel about that?'. This gives colleagues the opportunity to express constructive criticism: 'I am also pleased that we did it. However with all the overtime I had a lot of trouble with my family.' That sort of response should also be worth acknowledging: 'I am glad to have someone like you in the company who is aware of the problems. What makes you think that changes are possible here?'

Solution Focused criticism

Criticising conversations are challenging for both supervisors and colleagues:

> Senior management fear loss of motivation, reduced co-operation and offensive remarks. Colleagues fear being misunderstood, personally insulted or treated in an unfair way. Therefore colleagues should be encouraged to present their own point of view. Solution-focused criticising attempts to provide a balance of praise and criticism. It is not helpful to spend much time in justification or discussions about who is to blame. It is better to look at the goals and desires for the future. At the end of the conversation the colleague should have understood the following points clearly: the supervisor is dissatisfied with a concrete behaviour; in the future he wishes for a concrete positive state and he is confident that the colleague will find a solution.

> A criticising conversation should not be a revenge, but the beginning of a positive change. It is not meant to change the colleague but to obtain better results. In order to be content with the results of the conversation, the senior manager must not

accept meaningless statements such as: 'I will think about it …, I will try harder …'. Both sides must make concrete agreements.' (*Schmitz, Billen 2003:78*)

A Solution Focused view relieves you of too much responsibility as a supervisor. You do not have to offer a solution about how your colleague will do better in the future. Instead, your colleague takes the responsibility of finding a solution himself with which both of you can be satisfied.

If you praise your colleagues appropriately, it is easier for you to criticise. Both can be used to be more effective in guiding colleagues and both can be taught in training sessions for senior management. Feedback can be used as a form of dialogue: to tell others how I see them or to learn how others see me. Feedback can be a very effective instrument encouraging learning from concrete experience in the training room.

Training managers in Solution Focused criticism

Preparing the scene

During training sessions, there is always a participant in the training group who wants to practise a difficult criticising conversation. This might be a conversation in the past, which did not end in a satisfactory way for him. Or it might be a conversation he has to have in the future and for which he would like to be better prepared.

Supported by the trainer, the trainee develops individual goals for the conversation. This means finding suitable sentences, which are noted on the flip chart. The formulations are 'polished', until they really fit the situation and the style of the trainee. The trainee will state clearly what he wishes in his role as supervisor and what his colleague should do or change in the future. The sentence that begins with 'I want you to …' or 'I expect you to …' must really correspond to the style of the supervisor. The sentence with which the supervisor expresses his confidence that the colleague will find a solution also has to be very authentic. Experience shows that formulations suggesting that the colleague has the necessary competence are particularly suitable: 'You have probably already considered how you could change that. What do you suggest?'

When all goals are clearly formulated, the flip chart sheet is placed in a way that the trainee can see it during the role-play.

With simple props (table, seats etc.), the trainee builds a stage for the role-play. While doing that, other details are clarified: where and when will the conversation take place, how will it be held without disturbance from outside, how will it be introduced, how will the conversation partners be seated?

The trainee may select someone from the training group to take on the role of the colleague. For senior managers this role offers the chance to experience the criticising conversation from a neutral perspective. By listening to the trainee working on his goals, the colleague learns a lot about the situation and his role. Through some further questions he receives the information he still needs in order to be able to start role-playing.

Playing the scene

The trainer gives the starting signal and the situation is played as realistically as possible, with the trainee using the concrete behaviour and the exact statements he wants to try out. During the conversation, the trainee may need patience and perhaps to endure moments of 'solutionlessness' – maybe against his habitual style. Even if the colleague does not make satisfying suggestions, the trainee should remain friendly, steadfast and interested in the solutions he offers.

Solution Focused feedback

The trainer reminds the other participants that most people are inclined to evaluate each other's behaviour critically during role-plays. Most frequently they think about: 'What does not work?', 'What would I do completely differently?' or 'What do I not like?'.

While watching the role-play, they are told to direct their attention consciously towards the things which are working already.

They should observe how the trainee succeeds in giving Solution Focused criticism. Their observations should be so specific that they can report on them immediately after the role-play. In addition it is helpful for many observers to take notes. That is also recommended for the trainer, since feedback is most effective when expressed in concrete terms.

Now the trainer prepares the trainee for taking feedback:

- Listen calmly to the suggestions of observers and colleague.
- Do not comment on the feedback; nor defend your own procedure.
- Thank the feedback givers and choose the suggestions which are useful to take with you. Leave everything else behind.

A structured procedure has proved to be successful in giving feedback in this exercise. The trainer organises giving feedback with the following rules, strictly followed.

> First round (Observers):
> 'This is what we liked in the situation.' (Just praise, no hidden suggestions!)
> Second round (Colleague):
> 'This is what I liked in the situation.'
> Third round (Player, who tried out new behaviour)
> 'I will do this in the real situation again.'
> 'I will try to do this differently next time.'

In the fourth round, observers, colleagues and trainer make suggestions as to how the criticising conversation could go even better.

According to all experience this sequence leads to feedback that is given appreciatively and which is accepted effectively. These rules make it easier in the role-play and feedback in which many participants normally feel uncomfortable or embarrassed.

Dealing with difficulties

The role-play 'runs into the sand'; the players go round in circles

Before starting the role-play make it clear that either the trainee or the trainer is allowed to interrupt the role-play. The conversation does not have to work well first time. That would set the role-players under too much 'success pressure' and would restrain their playfulness and fun in experimentation. The quality of the conversation usually does not improve with time. Therefore, be prepared to conclude the role-play if you notice that the players cannot find a satisfactory end.

The trainee does not pursue his goals

In more than half of the training situations I experience, the trainee deviates clearly in the conversation from the goals which he had previously compiled with me. Above all the crucial sentence 'I want you to ...' was not said by many trainees. In this case it is helpful to consider in the concluding feedback together with trainee, colleague and observers how you can succeed in pursuing clearly one's goals and interests in a crucial conversation.

The feedback is exclusively positive, no critical suggestions are given

Depending upon culture and confidence in the training group it can happen that the observers give very cautious and/or exclusively positive feedback, even if constructive criticism would be better. Here the trainer can role-model. While I normally give precedence in feedback rounds to the observers, in this case I begin with simple observations and suggestions. Thus the ice is broken quickly and the observers join in with their own suggestions.

Solution Focused feedback rules

Below are suggestions for SF feedback rules which you can use in many training situations. It is very easy to organise and it is firstly focused on the successful parts of the training situation. It is an interactive game which includes all or at least many participants of the training group as players, co-players, observers and feedback givers. Feedback is given in a very appreciative way which makes it easy for the trainees to take away helpful suggestions.

Trying out new behaviour
Find agreement in your group about how you want to act differently in a situation in which you are dissatisfied.
Play the situation as realistically as possible with the behaviour and the statements you want to change.

Feedback
1. Round (Observers):
'This is what we liked in the situation.'
2. Round (Co-Player/s):
'This is what I / we liked in the situation.'
3. Round (Player, who tried out new behaviour)
'I will do this in the real situation again.'
'I will try to do this differently next time.'
4. Round (Observers and Co-Player/s):
'Do you (player) want any suggestions?'
Give suggestions – only if the player wants them!

Coping with suggestions
Listen calmly to the suggestions of Observers and Co-Player/s
Do not comment on the feedback; do not defend your own procedure.
Thank the feedback givers and choose the suggestions which are useful to take away with you. Leave everything else behind.

Acknowledgements

Important ideas in this article were developed together with Lilo Schmitz, University of Düsseldorf and Alasdair Macdonald, Carlisle, with whom I conducted a workshop at the SOL 2003 Conference in Bristol ('Using SF in practical communications and management training'). Many thanks to Veronica Hughes, Jenny Clarke and Alasdair Macdonald for 'polishing' the article.

References

Schmitz, Lilo 2000, 'Motivation und Empowerment. Das Milwaukee-Modell für die Führungspraxis,' in *Handbuch Personalentwicklung*, Köln, Fachverlag Deutscher Wirtschaftsdienst, Ergänzungslieferung August 2000, 1–64.

Schmitz, L and Billen B 2003, *Mitarbeitergespräche. Lösungsorientiert, Klar, Konsequent*, Verlag moderne industrie.

Biographical note

Dr. Peter Röhrig – I work as a Solution Focused consultant, trainer and coach – mainly in Germany. With my formal educational background as an economist and social psychologist I learned to look at figures and people at the same time and to support organisations in their challenging task to satisfy their customers and staff as well as their shareholders.

For more than 20 years I was a manager in different service organisations where I learned how hard it is to become a good boss. So – besides quality development – leadership training and coaching are the main areas I work in. Together with Lilo Schmitz and Birgit Billen I developed Solution Focused leadership training and the organisational parts of an 18 month training in Solution Focused counselling.

If you want to know more about the way I work and how to use Solutions Focused consulting in a business environment please contact me:

Dr. Peter Röhrig
Mehlem Institut für Qualitätsentwicklung
Office Bonn: Mainzer Str. 155, D-53179 Bonn
Office Cologne: Balthasarstr. 81, D-50670 Köln
0049-228-346614
peter.roehrig@mehlem-institut.de
www.mehlem-institut.de

Originally published in Organisations and People, Volume 10, Number 4, pages 63–68.

How to Improve your Tennis, your Management Skills and your Organisation's Results

Paul Z Jackson

Solutions Focus formed the basis of a major coaching programme with Walkers Snackfoods. This article presents research on the impact of the programme from the point of view of clients and consultants, and assesses how SF ideas contributed to the consulting process as well as to the final coaching model.

The tennis coach smacks another ball over the net, and – once again – I run a few steps, stretch, swing and wallop it back. We're doing what works. My tennis is improving. It's a miracle.

And the great thing about this coach is that he focuses only on what's going well. He notices what I'm doing right and takes a great interest in my shots that sing off the racket and whiz into the corners of the court.

It's almost as if he thinks I somehow know exactly what to do, without him having to tell me – as if I can find the answers myself. While I'd have made no such claims at the start of the session, it does appear to be working.

This is Solutions Focused tennis coaching, and it's great. And as a practitioner of Solutions Focus in organisations, I'm enjoying being on the receiving end for a change.

Coaching now comfortably straddles sport and industry, and I wanted to confirm that a Solutions Focus adds a valuable new dimension to the art of coaching in any context.

A year or so ago, I co-wrote the book *The Solutions Focus – The SIMPLE way to positive change*, with Mark McKergow. Together we work as The Solutions Focus, providing consultancy and training to organisations. Although the book was not aimed specifically at them, many coaches have attended our series of open training courses, and some of our clients have also chosen to introduce Solutions Focus in the guise of coaching.

Before writing the book, we had realised that Solutions Focus would lend itself readily to coaching situations in organisations – either for one-to-ones or for managers to coach teams.

And we caught part of the great wave of coaching along the way, holding one-to-one sessions with senior accountants, for example, on topics as varied as presentation skills and saving a career under threat. I've coached line managers on time-management, delegation, strategic planning and even improving cooking skills. Recently, I've been coaching entrepreneurs on how to take their businesses forward.

Perhaps equally interesting is our experience of taking the SF concept into a coaching programme to transform an entire company's worth of managers into better coaches.

Taking SF coaching into a training programme

Walkers Snackfoods wanted a programme that would develop coaching skills as a core competence, to help people learn faster through sharing knowledge and experience, and to improve their ability to manage during an ambitious programme to grow market share.

One of our associates Peter Hopkins, director of The Learning Bridge, won the pitch – against other leading coaching organisations (including sports-based coaching) – largely because of the individual responsiveness – and therefore flexibility – promised by the Solutions Focus approach.

While we had to exercise great patience in introducing the

programme to the organisation, the careful step-by-step development process proved valuable in the long run. There were, for example, many discussions with members of the HR team, as you might expect.

Less predictably, we ran two pilot programmes, one for an HR team, another for the entire senior management team. The latter was particularly tense for our team, as the entire future of the programme depended on their collective verdict half an hour after the course ended.

Fortunately, given one or two amendments to the design, we received a thumbs up, and the roll-out began. From the outset, the intention was to spot internal facilitators who would eventually train the programme themselves, and we engaged in coach talent-spotting each time we ran the course.

The basic programme is a two-day course for up to 24 participants, giving them a framework for learning and practising Solutions Focused coaching. The programme has now been running for more than 18 months, and more than 400 managers – including every member of the executive team – have attended.

As you'll see from the comments of those involved, it's been a successful programme at making useful, practical differences – and both solutions focus and coaching are now part of the culture.

What's different about this project?

There were differences in the process of working with the client organisation, with the nature of the model at the heart of the programme, and in the training itself.

1 Every consultancy and training brochure and website talks about tailoring the programme to the requirements of the client. Well, 'Bespoke' is built into the Solutions Focus model in the basic principle of 'Every Case Is Different', and in this case we were given exceptionally detailed guidance by the client.

Figure1 – Participants ponder the definition of coaching

This meant, for example, that the opening moments of the programme were choreographed minute by minute to include themed music, an inspirational video linking back to previous events that Walkers had held, and a presentation to participants outlining the compelling reasons for this programme now.

2 The biggest conceptual difference is that our model is Solutions Focused, not problem focused. Conventional coaching, for example, often starts from what you are doing wrong. Typically a coach will take time with you to analyse the barriers to performance. We begin with what's working well.

This principle applies not only to each individual coaching interaction, but also to the design of the project – one of the first workshops found out what was already happening in the organisation that this programme could build upon.

3 In the training itself, participants experienced both

approaches – problem-focused and Solutions Focused and explicitly discussed the differences. It's not that there's anything inherently wrong with exploring problems, it's just that doing so is not usually necessary in order to find a solution, nor the quickest route to a solution.

There is usually an 'A-Ha' moment when this life-changing realisation kicks in. Part of the facilitation effort is to appreciate that that moment occurs to different people at different times, and to accommodate the varying degrees of Solutions Focusedness that then result. One of the pleasures of the programme was to see everyone 'get it' to some extent, irrespective of their varying skill levels at then applying it as coaches.

How much expertise does the coach need in the performer's topic?

The SF approach builds on existing skills of each coach and performer in any coaching interaction. We found that in an organisation where often managers remain in role for less than a year, it was helpful for them to realise that they could confidently place responsibility for expertise in the hands of the Performer, with the coach being expert at coaching, not necessarily the topic.

One of the problems in many organisations is that a manager has less functional expertise than their staff, yet is still expected to coach. The SF coaching process works whether or not the coach knows precisely how to do what the performer is aiming to do.

This would be less successful with a tennis coach, when a few technical tips might be the quickest way to a performer's improvement – I recall the prompt 'bring your left hand across your body when you play a forehand, Paul' as being just as useful as my working out for myself how to time a swing to (near) perfection.

The SF model also allows the search for expertise for the performer to include the coach's functional expertise, in the radically useful guise of Know-How. Here, the coach might be asked to transfer pertinent knowledge – rather than the 'telling the performer what to do' used in much physical skills training or conventional management-by-command.

On this programme, they would share a story related to, say, time-management, decision-making or other coaching topic, and invite performers to extract the helpful elements for themselves.

Findings from research and experience

For the research interviews in this article, we asked:

What was important to Walkers about the programme?
What benefits are they now getting from it?
What did you like personally about the Solutions Focus aspects?
What was the best thing about the programme?
What single difference would you most like to have seen?
Any other comments?

The responses here are from:

Sarah Miles, HR director
Dee Jones, senior sales trainer
Angus MacIver, vice president – board member, research
Krish Seal, Head of the Sales Operations team
Carole Neville, Programme Director/Administrator
Peter Hopkins, director of The Learning Bridge, company that took the programme into Walkers and subsequently into PepsiCo Europe. Co-trainer on most of the modules.
Mark McKergow, from The Solutions Focus, co-designer, and deliverer of the pilot modules

Sarah Miles – Director, Human Resources

What was important to Walkers about the programme?

Lack of coaching was identified as big gap when creating a compelling employee proposition.

In our ever-competitive market place for talent, we needed to ensure our proposition was robust.

We also believed that given the age and service profile across the management population in WSF – sharing know-how would have huge competitive advantage.

What benefits are they now getting from it?

Our recent Organisational Health Survey scores showed improvement in level of coaching across the business.

Sharing know-how is the highest profile concept from the programme. We are using it in a variety of ways across the business (formal and informal).

What did you like personally about the Solutions Focus aspects?

It fits with our culture – e.g. 'no weakness – just opportunity'; but it also challenged us too, as we are a culture of feedback, e.g. 'Let me tell you what you should do!'.

What was the best thing about the programme?

Know-how sharing; and the concept of helping people build their own solutions.

What single difference would you most like to have seen?

The programme itself was very different to other learning events for WSF people, so sometimes people's judgement about content was clouded. Would have been very interested in discussing alternative methods of delivery e.g. self-learning, on the job coach, team learning.

Krish Seal – Head of the Sales Operations team

What was important to Walkers about the programme?

Sharing know how; investing time in people to challenge the way we do things.

What benefits are they now getting from it?

SMARTer objectives, better follow up.

What did you like personally about the Solutions Focus aspects?

End visualisation, breaking it down into chunks, sparkling moments, digging into personal motivations.

What was the best thing about the programme?

Simplicity of OSKAR model [Author's note: OSKAR is the name of our Solutions Focused coaching model].
What single difference would you most like to have seen?

Application from the top down.

Angus MacIver – vice president – board member, research

*What was important to Walkers about the programme? and
What benefits are they now getting from it?*

To make 'sharing know how' part of our business – it's OK to ask for help – we don't need to reinvent the wheel.

What did you like personally about the Solutions Focus aspects?

This is about solving real business issues – before they happen, not diagnosing them after they happen.

What was the best thing about the programme?

The process was memorable enough to be used easily.

What single difference would you most like to have seen?

Wouldn't change it really although I'd like our programmes to be led more by Walkers managers.

Mark McKergow – Trainers' perspective

What was important to Walkers about the programme?

At the design stage, it was fitting them precisely. For example, it drew on their existing experience of coaching, and built on that. We did a one-day workshop early on about what was already working.

What did you like personally about the Solutions Focus aspects?

It sidestepped a whole lot of stuff that could have wasted a lot of time. Many of the managers picked up on it really quickly – they understood the SF aspect – and knew what to overlook. The OSKAR model worked well.

What was the best thing about the programme?

I liked the idea of not letting it die in the training room. They got it out into the workplace with hats and so on, to make it live in the organisation.

Within the programme, there was lots of practice.

And we designed it with Accelerated Learning. It could be made boring, but it wasn't.

What single difference would you most like to have seen?

Not have them so involved in the micro-design of the programme. They wanted to debrief the pilot sessions before the dust had settled. But that's clients for you, and we should have ensured a more realistic design budget – especially time-wise.

Peter Hopkins – Account Holder and Trainer

What was important to Walkers about the programme?

Getting people to take it on board quickly. The business needed to retain staff and pass on the know-how and have people be better coaches, fast, to develop their people.

What benefits are they now getting from it?

It's been running nearly three years and is very successful. What makes it so is the design and the excellence of the OSKAR process.

Coaching wasn't in the culture before, and it is now. Hundreds of people have been through the programme and the model is being used, the terminology is heard.

Coaching is regarded as a legitimate process and essential tool for the development and growth of the company – growth of people and growth of profit.

What was the best thing about the programme?

The delivery has been good, and it's supported on the outside with lots of effort to make it happen in the workplace.

Dee Jones – senior sales trainer

What was important to Walkers about the programme?

It was apparent to us that people were really not getting the best out of their line. Managers were not passing on their know-how. We had recruitment issues and leaving issues, and were not getting the most out of people. Our Organisational Health Survey was telling us this loud and clear.

So we wanted Coaching for retention and for passing on of Know-how.

And the programme delivered a big basket of skills, which was rolled out across all functions.

What benefits are they now getting from it?

Our new programmes follow on from Coaching to Win, as something to hang our hat on. It's a springboard to the next stage, with people remembering OSKAR, Coachable Moments and two or three other elements. They can maintain this and fine-tune it.

What did you like personally about the Solutions Focus aspects?

Personally, I felt strongly that we should look forward rather than backward, so solutions focus was hugely attractive.

What was the best thing about the programme?

The one-to-one guided coaching sessions were really good. The guy I partnered still talks to me about how he's getting on, and it's created a bond between us. We both learned a lot from it – it opened new doors in our mind-set.

I was able to ask someone to do something that I'd been afraid to ask them, and no longer view it as a favour. I had that meeting, they said yes, and it was fine.

The best thing is It Works.

What single difference would you most like to have seen?

Perhaps a streamlining of the content. There was lots of practice and easy steps, but perhaps so much that people were not always clear what was the important bit.

People still talk about it and feel it has value.

Carole Neville – Programme Director/Administrator

What was important to Walkers about the programme?

- that we gave our Managers simple tools and concepts that they could quickly and easily use to coach their people day to day
- that we make a shift in mindset from: tell to coach, from feedback after an event to coaching before an event, increase the amount of recognition and celebration, from the manager taking ownership (the monkey) for the problem to the manager enabling their team to solve their own problems

What benefits are they now getting from it?

- increased greatly the amount of know-how sharing within and across functions
- we have moved our Organisational Health Survey scores on coaching significantly – demonstrating that more coaching is happening and having an impact on our people

What did you like personally about the Solutions Focus aspects?

- helps build self-belief within an individual and 'Instilling Self Belief' is one of our Values

What was the best thing about the programme?

- that the model and concepts were simple to learn and apply but have a big impact on the performer's ability and self-belief

What single difference would you most like to have seen?

– tools and guidance on sustaining and embedding coaching in the
  workplace

As you see from respondents' comments, the programme was well
received and Solutions Focused coaching has embedded itself into
the culture, with correspondingly improved scores on the coaching-
related questions in a recent attitude survey.

We learned that attention to detail in the design phase is important – to assure the client that their expectations stand a chance of
being met and to be ready for the onslaught of a rolling programme
every few weeks.

Equally, it proved useful to remain flexible within each running of
the course, and to be ready to redesign both between programmes
and even on the fly. On every run, at least one character emerged
with a question or a case scenario we hadn't seen before.

Above all, the success of the project hinged on us taking a positive, Solutions Focused view from the outset, confident that

- Participants would lend themselves willingly to becoming
  better coaches.
- Walkers would commit themselves to supporting the
  programme with executive team presence at every event,
  with full HR team involvement, and with worthwhile mate-
  rials to help keep the concepts in mind for programme
  graduates – mouse-mats, slogan-bearing scribble pads,
  coaching caps, etc.
- There would be sufficient coaching expertise within every
  group to demonstrate good practice that could spread
  readily to every participant within the short space of two
  days.

What's happened since

More recently, we have trained Walkers own trainers to deliver the programme, and have embarked on a similar arrangement with PepsiCo Europe. The programme develops and flourishes, and even my tennis continues to improve.

Reference

Jackson, Paul Z and McKergow, Mark (2002), *The Solutions Focus: The SIMPLE way to positive change*, London, Nicholas Brealey Publishing.

Biographical note

Paul Z Jackson designs and presents training and development courses for a wide range of corporate clients and public organisations. His company offers consultancy, facilitation, coaching and training.

He has presented at Ashridge, the London Actors Centre, at Bath Spa University College and many international conferences. As a journalist, senior producer with BBC Radio Light Entertainment and as founder of various comedy teams – including the More Fool Us improvisation squad – he has prompted a lot of laughter, on-stage and off, mostly intentionally.

A graduate of Oxford University (MA, Oxon), contributor to scholarly publications, he lives in St Albans. Books include *Impro Learning, 58 1/2 Ways To Improvise In Training, The Inspirational Trainer* and (with Mark McKergow) *The Solutions Focus.*

Contact Paul on, +44 1727 843820, paul@impro.org.uk

Originally published in Organisations and People, Volume 10, Number 4, pages 69–76.

Dreams do Come True – with a little help from Discovery, Dreaming, Design and Delivery

Patricia Lustig

Sometimes an 'organisation' may not be a corporation or a team, but a town or village. Here Patricia Lustig describes her experience of using Appreciative Inquiry under challenging conditions in Nepal.

I had a dream that there would be some way to help the people in the small Nepalese community of Phakhel that wouldn't require masses of foreign (i.e. from outside the village) help. Didn't know how I was going to do it, but I knew I would and I thought Ai (Appreciative Inquiry) might hold the key!

I first voiced this dream in the summer of 1998 and in November of that year met Mac Odell. He had adapted Ai to work with villagers so that we ran a sort of mini-4D cycle (Discovery, Dreaming, Design and Delivery) in 2 hours (which is all the time these subsistence level farmers had to give us). We trained and worked with a few consultants he was planning to use on a USAID-funded project ... in the event they didn't use it further at that time. This was exactly what I needed for Phakhel so I got some of my Nepali colleagues enthused and we went off to try it out.

To start out with, most villagers see white skin and ask for money, but in Phakhel, where I was well known, they were just curious about sharing learning and about discovering what it was that I actually DO.

There was a core group of people who were almost always there when we had our meetings (every few months), but otherwise we just worked with whoever showed up. I was later asked to work with the next village as well. Basically, I came about three times a year and met with the villagers and helped them with the process and when they got stuck, helped to un-stick them.

We separated the men, women and children into different groups and came together to share information. Did it change the dialogue in the village? Definitely! One man got up to say, 'This really brings it home to me. We've been bloody lazy! For the past 40 years we have been holding our hands out for aid from the government and what do we get? We fight, we can't agree on anything and we don't feel good about ourselves. Forty years ago, we did a lot together because there was no one else to help us and you know what? We were proud of what we did! We were proud of our village. Are any of you proud now? No? Well, let's do this together and be proud again!'

And, of course, they are doing it. It took some time for them to get used to the methodology, but it is easy enough to 'crank the crank' as it were. The problems for sustainability arise when they encounter obstacles. Unless there is someone with them who is trained in facilitation skills, they get entrenched in old and familiar behaviour patterns and get stuck. At present, this is not the case for the school project, but when it happens, they have asked me to come back. In the meantime, they operate on their own without outside interference.

The methodology we used was as follows:

Discovery was asking them to tell us a story about something that had gone well in the village, which they had done together. We had them draw on flip chart paper because most of them were illiterate. Extra time was necessary in the beginning to get the women to even pick up a pen!

Dreaming was asking them what kind of a village they would like for their children and grandchildren, again getting them to draw.

Design was more difficult, we asked them to plan … and discovered that people who couldn't read didn't seem to have developed the logical sides of their brains enough … they didn't know how to plan, so this had to be taught! (It took a while for me to figure this out. I didn't understand why they couldn't do it … I was using the right word, I knew I was. They knew what it meant, but not how to DO it). We worked simply, beginning with prioritising what had to come first, then setting out steps and identifying obstacles and what kind of organisation might be needed. To teach how to plan, we worked with things they were already doing (like when to plant their crops and the steps they needed to take) and built upon that.

Finally came **Delivery** – except this sort of got stuck onto the Design work. When they came back to report on the Design, they all stood up and went straight into who committed to do what. It was quite marvellous.

What can we do right now? This is important and is a step that Mac added. If we all do something together in five or ten minutes, it gives everyone a good feeling and people see how much can be achieved in a short time if everyone helps.

Then we do a debrief, and finally we get people to dance and sing, to give a fun memory of the work they have done.

The villagers raised 34,000 Rupees (a phenomenal amount for a community of 88 families where the average income of a family of six is about 10,000 Rupees per year) and had sunk the school foundations when I visited them in May 2000. They then built upon the foundations (these needed to stabilise during monsoon). And guess what?!

1. They have received a grant from PLAN International to build the first model secondary school. The grant is 2.2 million Rupees. The school will have 14 classrooms on two

floors. When I visited in March 2001, the first floor was finished. PLAN heard what they were doing and knew they were onto a winner. Like everyone else, they want to be successful, so why not follow success?

2. The villagers have now raised in excess of 162,000 Rupees themselves! This money goes for the registration fee (secondary schools are not provided by the government and they require a fee of 50,000 Rupees for registration), which has already been paid, and for paying the teachers' salaries and buying equipment and books, as the government does not support secondary schools in any way. Teachers would earn on average between 4,000 and 8,000 Rupees per month.

They seem to move from strength to strength with this. What I am being told indicates a strong community organisation behind this work, led by an unmarried lady in her forties, a 70-year-old grandfather and another gentleman in his forties who does have children, now attending secondary school far away from home in Kathmandu.

In *this* case and for *this* project it has truly become sustainable. Let us admire and appreciate what the villagers have done!

We did produce a short 4-minute film of the process in Phakhel, which is available in the UK for £9.99 (including VAT and P & P within the UK), so if anyone is interested I'd be delighted to send them a copy while they last.

Bibliographical note

Patricia Lustig is Managing Director of LASA Development UK Ltd., an international consultancy group. She works at all levels and has exceptional experience with understanding of European and Asian cultures where she advises national and international organisations, both in the profit and the not-for-profit sector. She specialises in the use of Appreciative Inquiry (Ai) as a change methodology and is particularly interested in developing the next generation of Ai practice, linking Ai into the creative process. She is a Member of the IOD and a Founder Member of UKCLC. She is also an Associate of Bath Consultancy Group and a member of the nowherecommunity.

Originally published in AMED News, February 2001

Reviews

Authentic Happiness

Using the New Positive Psychology to Realise Your Potential for Lasting Fulfilment

MARTIN SELIGMAN
Published by Nicholas Brealey Publishing, 2003
Paperback £15.00
ISBN 1857883292

Psychology is taking a positive turn

Until recently psychology has mainly been working within a disease model: a strong emphasis has been placed on discovering deficits in human behaviour and finding ways to repair this damage. Psychologists hardly focused on doing studies acquiring knowledge about healthy functioning and building strengths. In other words: they have focused solely on taking away something negative (the disfunctioning) instead of adding something positive (increasing mental and behavioural health). The result: psychologists know little about healthy and happy functioning. This situation has been changing now since the rise of positive psychology a few years ago. What is Positive Psychology? It is a new movement in psychology, originated by Martin Seligman and a few other prominent psychologists, among them Mihali Csikszentmihalyi (author of 'Flow'). It aims to be a psychological science about the best things in life. Main topics of study are: positive emotions, positive traits and positive institutions. This book, *Authentic Happiness,* is the first book on positive psychology. Seligman is its main spokesperson.

Happiness

This book mainly deals with the phenomenon of happiness. According to Seligman your enduring level I happiness results from three factors: your *'set range'* (the basic biologically determined range within which your happiness normally will be), the *'circumstances of your life'* (some conditions – like being married and living in a democratic country-somehow seem to contribute to happiness), and your *'voluntary control'* (the things you can do to get your happiness to the upper part of your set range). OK, but how to get this done? Before answering this question Seligman explains that happiness/positive emotion can refer to three domains: the past (satisfaction, contentment, fulfilment, pride and serenity), the present (joy, ecstasy, calm, zest, ebullience, pleasure and flow) and the future (optimism, hope, faith, trust). Then the author comes up with suggestions to improve your happiness:

How to increase your happiness

1) To be happier about your past, you need to: a) let go of the false belief that your past negative experiences determine your present and future, b) increase your gratitude about the good things in your past and c) learn how to forgive past wrongs.

2) To be happier in your present, you need to distinguish between pleasures and gratifications. Pleasures are delights that have clear sensory and strong emotional components that require little if any thinking. Gratifications are flow-experiences. They are activities we very much like doing but that are not necessarily accompanied by any raw feelings at all. The gratifications last longer than the pleasures and they are underpinned by our strengths and virtues. The key to happiness in past and future lies in enhancing gratifications.

3) To be happier about your future, you need to change your explanatory style in order to become more optimistic and

hopeful (this links back to Seligman's previous book, *Learned Optimism*).

Using your strengths

These explanations imply what Seligman means by Authentic Happiness. He says we should not rely on shortcuts like television watching, chocolate eating, loveless sex, and buying things to feel happy. He explains that positive emotion alienated from the exercise of character leads to emptiness, to inauthenticity, and to depression. So we want to feel like we deserved our positive feelings. That's why Seligman says Authentic Happiness comes from identifying and cultivating your most fundamental strengths and using them every day in work, love, play, and parenting. This message reminds me of Czsikszentmihalyi's 'Finding Flow'.

Core virtues and strengths

Psychology has devised a classification system (i.e. a language) for describing abnormal behaviour and mental diseases. But it lacked a language describing human effectiveness and sanity. That is why Seligman and a team of scholars researched sources from all kinds of cultures and times in history and found that there is a strong convergence in what these traditions consider to be virtues and strengths. This led to the formulation of a classification system of virtues and strengths: Six Core Virtues: 1) Wisdom and knowledge, 2) Courage, 3) Love and humanity, 4) Justice, 5) Temperance, 6) Spirituality and transcendence. Further they identified 24 strengths corresponding to these virtues. This book contains definitions of this taxonomy and some questionnaires for the reader to complete (the questionnaires can be found on the web too, by the way: www.authentichappiness.org).

The book is pleasantly written. Seligman writes in a rather personal and honest style, which makes the book lively (for instance he exclaims on page 24: 'I am a hideous example of my own theory.')

I recommend this book to anyone interested in psychology and in happiness (although it is not a self-help book in the first place, I think). The book ends reflectively dealing with the relationship between positive emotions and win-win situations, and speculating that we may be on the threshold of an era of win-win games and feeling good. I enjoyed reading the book and I like positive psychology. It is in many ways reminiscent of humanistic psychology (which I always liked) but has a more scientific approach. I am optimistic it will be a success.

Coert Visser
http://www.m-cc.nl

The Skaleboard

SOLUTIONSURFERS
Coaching resource
£105 plus £5 shipping
www.solutionsurfers.com

The 'Skaleboard' developed by Peter Szabó of SolutionSurfers is a tangible tool for coaching and management visualising scales in Solution Focused coaching conversations. It can be used by coaches, managers, and anyone dealing with change and improvement in one-to-one conversations.

In contrast to what the name suggests, the 'Skaleboard' is a rather handy A4 format (anyone thinking that they would have to manoeuvre a surfboard into the meeting room can rest assured – it will fit into a briefcase). There are 5 neutral scales from 1 to 10 on a magnetic board with 10 multi-coloured magnets for marking points on the scales and moving them around. The 'Skaleboard' comes with a writing pad of the same design, so you can label the scales and mark the results on paper for your coachee to take home and for use in a future coaching.

Using a 'Skaleboard' might seem a bit redundant when you can also scale progress or future possibilities by saying a number between one and ten or by jotting down a number of scales on a piece of paper. Here are some of the advantages that emerged in interviews with users and in my own coaching using the 'Skaleboard':

When you use scales without visualisation, you are normally limited to two or three scales in a conversation depending on how good you and your coachee are with numbers. With a 'Skaleboard', it is easy to 'surf' 5 scales simultaneously and thus handle interdependencies in complex issues.

Another important advantage of using the 'Skaleboard' is that it provides an environmental cue for 'reflection time'. As a manager, you lead very different types of conversations from small talk at the coffee machine to termination conversations. Pulling out a 'Skaleboard' signalises that the conversation you are going to have will be structured, Solution Focused, and aimed at learning.

Being able to push a little magnet up and down a scale is also a different experience from marking a point on a piece of paper. Your client can test more tentatively where on the scale would be just right for him or her. When coaching with the 'Skaleboard', clients generally take more responsibility for their coaching progress possibly because they themselves are moving the 'counters' around.

The manual to the 'Skaleboard' supplies examples of most frequently used scales: the progress scale, the confidence scale, the learning scale, and the motivation scale and two set of cards with questions for an entire session: 'Solution Talk' going through the phases of a Solution Focused coaching from 'future perfect' to 'small steps' and 'Performance Appraisal', 12 questions for a solution oriented performance review. However, the 'Skaleboard' can be used for all kinds of scales and conversations and users are encouraged to adapt it to their respective situations.

Kirsten Dierolf
Kirsten@kirsten-dierolf.de

The Solutions Focus

The SIMPLE Way to Positive Change

PAUL Z JACKSON AND MARK McKERGOW
Published by Nicholas Brealey Publishing (2002)
Paperback £16.99
ISBN 1857882709

Looking for a different kind of consultancy

Several years ago I left a major consultancy firm to start my own little consultancy. I had not been happy for quite some time with the traditional ways of working within consultancy, which I had observed to be ineffective very often, and was determined to do things differently. The only problem was I did not precisely know how. I had reflected on which had been my best and most successful moments as a consultant and came to the following conclusion. I had been most successful when I asked my clients what they wanted to achieve, listened a lot, asked a lot of questions, checked if I had understood my clients right, listened more, asked more questions etc. My confusion was great, what kind of consultancy was *this*?

Applying the Solution Focus in organisations

Then a colleague of mine told me about Solution Focused Brief Therapy. This was a brilliant approach making it possible to make therapy more respectful and effective. It resembled how I wanted to work as a consultant. My colleague and I were convinced that the principles behind it were quite applicable in management coaching and in quite a lot of other sub-fields of consultancy as well. We read almost everything there was on the topic (which was almost entirely focused on therapy) and started to apply it in our work as organisational consultants. It felt like pioneering. We experienced it as a highly positive, pragmatic and effective approach, which is highly applicable in the world of business.

Mark McKergow and Paul Z Jackson

After some time we discovered two English guys who were travelling on the same road: Mark McKergow and Paul Z Jackson. Only, I hate to admit, they were several miles ahead of us ... They had a great website, they had started an international network of SF consultants, had started a mailing list, and delivered Solution Focused training programmes. We were thrilled and impressed. And then they published *The Solutions Focus: The S.I.M.P.L.E Way to Positive Change*. We expected the book to be great and we were right.

The SIMPLE way

This great book clearly and pleasantly describes the basics of working Solution Focused: first define your goals and then move directly toward them, without looking for problem causes, by focusing on finding out what works and doing more of that. If something does not work, stop doing it and try something else. The authors have found a very suitable acronym to explain the basics of the solution focus: SIMPLE: **S**olutions – not problems, **I**nbetween – the action is in the interaction, **M**ake use of what's there – not what isn't, **P**ossibilities – past, present and future, **L**anguage – simply said, **E**very case is different – beware ill-fitting theory. The acronym is terrific because it captures the most essential elements of the Solution Focus well and at the same time points at an important feature of the Solution Focus: that it is simple. But, no matter how simple it may be, the authors stress that to practise it, you do need quite some skills and discipline. They explain it can be especially hard to resist the temptation to go back to analysing problems.

Practical and profound

This book, which, to my knowledge is the first English book on applying the Solution Focus in organisations, is both practical and profound. Besides presenting the principles simply and in a lively manner, it also goes into some backgrounds in a brief and to the point manner. The solution focus is compared and related to approaches like Appreciative Inquiry, NLP, Complexity theory and the work on flexible optimism by Martin Seligman. And I loved to read the description of Occam´s Razor, of the Bavelas experiment and how raw sewage (!) helped cure infections. Please don't worry if this last part sounds too theoretical. The book is very practical in that it provides helpful tools and interesting and very recognisable and sometimes funny cases.

Conclusion: one of the first two books I would recommend

For anyone interested in the Solution Focus this book would be one of the first two books I would recommend first (the other one being: *Interviewing for Solutions* by Peter De Jong and Insoo Kim Berg, Wadsworth, 2001). I am very pleased with this book – it has been a great help in applying SF in organisations. I will bet: if you read this book, you will start applying at least parts of what you have read.

Coert Visser
http://www.m-cc.nl

Solution Focused Coaching: Managing people in a complex world

JANE GREENE and ANTHONY M GRANT
Published by Pearson Education, Harlow
Softback, 177 pages,
ISBN 1 843 04028 X

Written by an academic and a practitioner, this is more than a coaching manual with an emphasis on solution approaches. It is good on theory, background and benefits, and the importance of coaching for both individuals and organisations in today's fast changing environment. Clearly written, and well presented, pages throughout are littered with highlighted examples, case studies, and research findings. Important ideas and passages are picked out and set out with an *in-your-face* boldness that makes it an excellent reference to revisit and dip into.

At one level, all good coaching is solution or goal orientated but, at its best, Solution Focused thinking enables people to tap into the wealth of experiences, skills, expertise and intuition they possess. This may seem a subtle shift but at the deeper level it can mean a complete reframing of perceptions. Our cause and effect orientated western culture seems to distrust intuition as it continues to seek to eradicate problems. Often this merely perpetuates the difficulties. Yet, the authors point out, the natural sciences now suggest understanding causes does not always allow the prediction of effects. Concentrating on problems can make us feel worse; a solution mindset immediately shifts the why? to how to — from the past to the future.

Greene and Grant start by looking at coaching from a complexity theorists viewpoint, and how an individual reframing problems can have huge leverage within whole organisations. The remainder sets out to inform the reader on some of the techniques and tools that can be applied. They revisit the GROW model and some of its modifications, and look at feedback, communication, questioning, listening, rethinking and reframing. There is a short chapter on the change models of Lewin, Bridges, and Prochaska and DiClemente, and they assess the benefits of coaching in-house and becoming a 'manager-coach'.

Much of the book is based on research from the Coaching Psychology Unit, at Sydney University. As Jackson and McKergow point out in their book (see review above), combined with solutions, coaching proves a potent mix and this book is a welcome addition to the growing library of Solution Focused guides.

Terry Gibson
Editor, Organisations and People

Reviews originally published in Organisations and People, Volume 10, Number 4, pages 77–79.

ASSOCIATION for MANAGEMENT EDUCATION AND DEVELOPMENT

AMED is a network for professional managers, academics and consultants interested in the development of people and organisations.

The association seeks to promote the exchange of insights, ideas and best practice in the field if individual and organisation development.

AMED's aim is to foster the development of people and organisations. Its style, reflecting this aim, is development with the emphasis on self-development. Members of **AMED** gain access to an extensive network of individuals, a regular newsletter, the international quarterly journal *Organisations & People*, and a range of conferences, workshops and development opportunities. In addition, members create a wide range of other benefits out of the opportunities that **AMED** provides.

In surveys of members, the benefits arising from AMED activities have clustered around six main areas:

- being in touch with the leading edge
- developing professional skills
- extending professional networks
- making friends with like-minded people
- business networking
- impacting on developments in management and organisation development

The character of **AMED** is formed by its members. The values that underpin its life grow and change as members grow and change. How members liaise and network with one another is the association's lifeblood.

The benefits of membership thus arise out of the energy and interests of those who join **AMED**. It is an association for people who are professionally interested in the education and development of themselves, other people, and organisations. Its members create what they want in order to enhance their abilities as developers and to explore the national and international questions surrounding development in our time.

AMED offers scope for life-long membership. Since development needs change through life, what members want will change through their lives too: different modes of involvement at different times. You choose what you want. If what you want doesn't already exist you can remedy that!!

Further information about AMED and membership details is available from:

AMED   *Phone: +44 (0)1480 493253*
34 The Broadway   *Fax: +44 (0)1480 493259*
St Ives   *Email: amedoffice@amed.org.uk*
Huntingdon   *Website: www.amed.org.uk*
Cambridge
PE27 5BN
UK

Organisations & People

O & P is an authoritative quarterly journal of the UK based *Association for Management Education and Development* **(AMED)** which has gained an enviable reputation throughout the English speaking world and Europe. Its target audience is the reflective practitioner which includes managers with responsibility for the development of organisations and individuals – such as strategists and line managers – as well as in-house and consultant organisation and management developers.

It aims to form an effective link between the world of academic advance and the practitioner whose business results may be influenced significantly by the success or otherwise of development initiatives.

The editors of O & P have set out to ensure articles combine intellectual rigour with high readability while presenting high-grade material in a style that is easily accessible to those at all stages of their business career.

Articles are written by practitioners for practitioners. Any subject within the broad range of developing organisations and individuals is acceptable and in the past have included: case studies of practical problems when enabling managers to take on the task of coaches to their staff, change management, cultural diversity, whole system development, complexity and other topical areas relevant to development.

Articles can, on request, be peer reviewed by either a panel of practitioners or a panel of academics from around the world. Occasional academic articles reflecting current research are welcomed as long as they are written with practitioners in mind.

Inquiries about submitting prospective articles should be sent to terry@amed.org.uk.

AMED is an educational charity and cannot pay authors for submissions. It is a mark of the esteem in which the journal is held that a constant stream of articles is submitted.

All articles published in O & P become the property of **AMED**, but authors have full rights to alter their own material and republish elsewhere on condition that **AMED** and O & P are attributed. Articles should be around 3500 words and of a quality and standard for a professional journal. Longer articles may be accepted at the discretion of the editors.

O & P is a subscription journal and part of AMED membership services. However, sale of the journal to non-members is encouraged.

Further details about O & P can be found on the Publications pages of the AMED website: www.amed.org.uk.

How to subscribe to Organisations & People

Send your name and address to amedoffice@amed.org.uk with a request to make arrangements for setting up a non-member subscription.

ABOUT SOL

Solutions in Organisations Linkup
Sharing and building Solutions Focused practice in organisations

SOL organises conferences and events around the world to help people join the growing movement to use Solutions Focused ideas at work, in consulting, managing, training, HR practice, strategic planning, performance management, team building and organisational development. The first conference was in February 2002 in Bristol, UK, hosted by Bristol Solutions Group.

For us, sharing is the key word. The originators of the approach, Steve de Shazer and Insoo Kim Berg, have not trade marked their work. Indeed, the SF approach itself is based on collaboration.

It is important to us that SOL retains this generosity of spirit and the collaborative ethos. No-one owns the Solutions in Organisations Link-up name. We do not favour a membership based organisation with the corresponding administrative costs and duties. SOL is not a membership organization. You can join in by participating in SOL events, and/or joining the SOL email discussion group listserver, SOLUTIONS-L.

SOL is run voluntarily by an international steering group. The group meets at SOL International Conferences - if you are interested in getting involved, come to a conference, or contact one of the group in advance.

Anyone is free to organize an event under the SOL banner, as long as it is in line with the SOL Charter and has the support of the international steering group. If you have an idea for an event, whether it be geographically based (ie a national or regional event) or subject-matter oriented (focusing on a particular application of solution focused work), get in touch with any member of the steering group via

www.solworld.org

The new wave of change continues in SolutionsBooks!

Team Coaching with the SolutionCircle
A Practical Guide to Solutions Focused Team Development

by Daniel Meier

ISBN 0-9549749-1-3

'Daniel has done a formidable job; a service for anyone who is seriously interested in working with teams in a solution-focused manner. The book gives you the steps of the dance. Follow these steps and you will be amazed how this simple – yet profound – approach can help you help teams achieve their goals in ways that are not only effective but fun at the same time.'

Ben Furman
Helsinki Brief Therapy Institute, inventor of the Reteaming method

www.solutionsbooks.com

Index

4–Ds model 7, 101–102, 155
Abbotson, Sue 93, 105
action description 114, 117
affirm/affirmation 68, 70–71, 73, 77
Association for Management Education and Development (AMED) ix, xiii, 171–175
Andersen, Tom 67, 76, 78
appraisal 9, 81–82, 84–92, 125, 165
appraisal interviews 81–82, 87–90
appreciation 28–31, 33–34, 36, 49, 90
appreciative inquiry (Ai) xiii, 1–2, 5–11, 25, 27–30, 33, 36, 93–95, 98, 101–102, 105, 155, 158, 168
appreciative organisation 31–33

Bakhtin, Mikhail 5
Barrett, F J 28, 36
Bateson, Gregory 8
Berg, Insoo Kim 8, 10, 53, 65, 87, 92, 110–114, 116, 119, 128, 168, 175
Bernardin, J 81–82, 92
boundarying 42
Bristol Solutions Group 67, 78, 175
Buckingham, Marcus & Clifton, Donald O 3–4, 10

Cameron, Esther 42, 50
Carrell, M 81, 92
Cauffman, Louis 13, 22–23, 110–111, 119
clarifying/clarification 14, 20, 68–69, 71, 73, 75, 104, 110
client-directed 121, 125–126
closing 68, 70–71, 74
coaching 9–10, 13–15, 22, 40, 68, 78, 92, 102, 110, 119, 128, 139, 141–154, 164, 166, 169–170, 175
  conventional 144
  Solutions Focused 14–15, 110, 128, 164–165, 169
  systemic 102, 105
coachulting 13
Coens, T & Jenkins, M 82, 92
competency management 121–122, 124–127
complaints 17, 43
compliments 17, 68, 70, 73, 75–77
confusion 127
conjoint relations 27, 29
constellations, organisational 93–94, 105
consulting 1, 13, 22, 68, 79, 140, 141, 175

conventional coaching 144
conventional psychology 1, 3
conventional wisdom 2
conversation 5, 15–16, 19, 22, 26–28, 30, 33, 35–36, 53, 62–65, 125, 131, 133–137, 164–165
  Solutions Focused xiv, 131
Cooperider, David 6–7, 10, 28, 36
coping questions 112–113
counters 58, 165
criticism, SF 133–134, 136
Cunningham, I 72, 78
customer orientation 83–85
Czikszentmihalyi, Mihalyi 4, 161, 163

de Jong, Peter 8, 10, 87, 92,112, 114, 119, 128, 168
delivery phase 102, 157
demotivation 86, 88
de Shazer, Steve 8, 10, 18, 77–78, 87, 92, 175
design phase 101, 157
development 125, 131, 139, 143, 171–176
differences 3, 9, 26, 31–32, 34, 54, 56, 61, 63, 86–88, 104, 143, 145
differentiation 17, 20–22
discovery phase 95, 98, 101, 156
Dolan, Yvonne 44, 50
dreaming phase 157
Drucker, Peter 5

effectiveness scale 60–61
enterprise support group (ESG) 74
Erickson, Milton 8
evaluation 31–33, 81–82, 108, 116
excellence 61, 96
exceptions 16–17, 20, 56, 90, 124
exception-finding questions 111, 114, 118

facilitation 50–51, 109, 116, 145, 154, 156
Falk Team, The 76–77
feedback 31, 71, 75, 77, 81, 94, 100, 107, 112, 116, 131–132, 134–138, 147, 152, 169
  positive 75, 77, 132, 137
  Solutions Focused 131, 135, 138
future 4, 25, 28–29, 33, 37, 39, 46, 48–49, 55, 57, 63, 71, 77, 81, 83, 90–91, 94, 97, 100, 103, 107–111, 114–116, 123, 133–134, 143, 162, 164–165, 167, 169

future orientation 18–21, 110
future perfect 57, 165

Gallwey, Timothy 57, 65
Gergen, Kenneth 5, 10, 27, 35–36
Glasgow Group 111, 119
goal-setting 15, 19, 21, 113
Grant, Anthony xiv, 169
Greene, Jane xiv, 169
GROW model 169

Hammond, Sue Annis 8, 10, 28, 36
happiness 3–6, 10, 161–164
Hellinger, Bert 97, 105
Henden, John 39, 51
Hjerth, Michael 67, 71, 75–76, 78
Hunt, John 4

inductive approach 123
insight 17, 56, 72, 94–95, 98, 102–104, 171
instruments, rating 81, 83, 85–86, 88
interactional approach 5, 75, 125
internal others 27
interview techniques 89–90
interviews, appraisal 81–82, 87–90
interviews/interviewing 8, 10, 75–76, 81, 83–84, 86–92, 98, 124, 146, 165
  Solutions Focused 75, 88

Jackson, Paul Z xiv, 9–11, 42, 50, 57, 65, 91–92, 111, 128, 141, 154, 166–167, 170

know-how 145, 147, 150–152

leaders, organisational 25–26, 94
learning contract 72
learning sets 68, 72–74
life, organisational 4–5, 25, 28–31, 35
Lueger, Günter 81, 92
Lustig, Patricia 9–10, 93, 105, 155, 158

McKergow, Mark xiv, 1, 9–11, 42, 50, 57, 65, 91–92, 111, 128, 142, 146, 149, 154, 166–167, 170
McNamee, Sheila 25, 36–37
Mental Research Centre 8
mentoring 68
Miller, Scott D 44, 50, 112–113, 116, 119

Mintzberg, H 109, 112, 120
Miracle Question, The 18–19, 46, 111, 113–114, 117
Moreno's psychodrama 94
Mortensen, Jim 107, 120
motivation 17, 26, 53, 132–133, 139, 148, 165
multiple voices 32
Murphy, K 82, 92

neurolinguistic programming (NLP) 2, 8, 10, 168
Norman, Harry 67, 74, 78
not knowing 18, 123

Occam's Razor 8, 168
O'Hanlon, W H 71, 78, 110, 120
organisation, appreciative 31–33
organisational constellations 93–94, 105
organisational leaders 25–26, 94
organisational life 4–5, 25, 28–31, 35
organisational practices 26–27, 29, 31
organisational transformation (OT) 93, 95, 97, 102
orientation, customer 83–85
future 18–21,110
OSKAR 148–151

participant buy-in 111
participatory practices 32
performance appraisal 9, 60, 81–82, 90–92, 165
performance improvement 53, 57
Pidsley, Tim 67, 73, 78–79
platform 95
positive approach 1–3, 10
positive feedback 75, 77, 132, 137
positive psychology xiii, 2–3, 6, 161, 164
practices, organisational 26–27, 29, 31
participatory 32
praise 131–134, 136
presenting 68–69, 71
problem talk 43, 50, 73, 88–89
progress, scale of 17
psychology, conventional 1, 3
positive xiii, 2–3, 6, 161, 164
psychotherapy 1, 78

questions, coping 112–113
exception-finding 111, 114, 118
solution-building 13, 15–16, 19, 22

rater training 90–91
rating instruments 81, 83, 85–86, 88

rating, Solutions Focused 81, 86, 91–92
reflecting 68, 70–71, 73, 76–78
relational practice 27, 33–34
relations among groups 27, 29–30
remotivation 39–40
resources 8, 16, 20, 27–28, 36, 44, 49, 56, 67–69, 75, 83, 87, 101, 108, 110, 132, 146
hunting for 16, 20
Röhrig, Peter 131, 139–140
Rossi, Kendy 9–10
Royal, C 28, 36

Sampson, E E 27, 36
scales 53, 55–56, 58, 62–63, 81, 83, 85, 87, 164–165
scaling 53–54, 56–58, 61–62, 65, 117
scalingboard 56
scaling questions 53–54, 56–59, 62, 64–65, 111, 114–115, 117
Schein, Ed 1, 10
Schlundt Bodien, Gwenda 121, 123–124, 128–129
self-managed learning 67, 72
Seligman, Martin xiv, 3–4, 10–11, 161–163, 168
SFR teams 67–68, 71–77
Sharry, John 46, 50
Skaleboard xiv, 56, 164–165
social construction 5–6, 10, 25–28, 30–31, 37
socialising 14
solution-building questions 13, 15–16, 19, 22
Solution Focused Brief Therapy (SFBT) xi, 8, 22, 50, 109, 166
Solutions Focus xi, xiii–xiv, 1–2, 5–6, 8–11, 13–14, 42, 50, 53, 56, 58, 63, 65, 67, 81, 92, 107, 110–112, 116–119, 121, 124, 128, 140–149, 151–154, 166–167, 175–176
Solutions Focused coaching 14–15, 110, 128, 164–165, 169
Solutions Focused conversation xiv, 131
Solutions Focused criticism 133–134, 136
Solutions Focused feedback 131, 135, 138
Solutions Focused interviewing 75, 88
Solutions Focused principles 9
Solutions Focused rating 81, 86, 91–92
Solutions Focused reflecting teams (see also SFR teams) xiii, 67
Solutions Focused scaling, principles of 53, 56–57
Solutions Focused training 167

Solutions in Organisations Link-up (SOL) ix, xiv, 51, 139, 175
SolutionsBooks xi, xii–xiii, 175
Srivastva, Suresh 6–7, 36
stability, assumption of 83, 85
Steiner, Therese 53, 65
strategic planning 9, 107–113, 115–120, 142, 175
strengths 3–5, 10, 33, 44, 49–50, 89, 93, 101, 108, 111, 123, 125, 128, 161–163
sustainable transformation 95–96
systemic behaviour 97
systemic coaching 102, 105
systemic process 30–31
systemic swim 27
Szabó, Peter 53, 66, 164

teams 8–9, 58–59, 64, 67–68, 71–78, 125, 142, 154
time line 47–49
Time Quake 45–46
tools, of conventional psychology 3
training 2, 9, 16–17, 53, 66, 68, 74, 90–91, 117–120, 150, 152–153, 164, 168–169
transformational 98
traditional approach v. appreciative approach 32, 89–90
traditional models and methods 16, 25, 31–33, 68, 88–90, 102, 166
traditional rating instruments 83, 85–86
training 2, 4, 8, 51, 66, 68, 72, 75, 81, 90–91, 116, 131, 134–135, 137–139, 142–144, 146, 149, 154, 167, 175
rater 90–91
Solutions Focused 167
transformation 93, 95–98, 102
insight-led 102
organisational 93, 95, 97, 102
principles for 96–97
sustainable 95–96

Visser, Coert 121, 123–125, 128–129, 164, 168

Walkers Snackfoods programme 141–154
Watkins, Jane McGruder & Mohr, Bernard J 7, 11
Weiner-Davis, Michelle 110, 120
Whitney, Diana 7, 10
Wilk, J 71, 78
wisdom, conventional 2
Wittgenstein, Ludwig 5, 27, 36